RAIL CENTRES:
BRISTOL

Title page:
Numberless and nameless 4-6-0s by St Philip's Marsh coaling stage, 6 February 1964. Right to left: No 5050 *Earl of St Germans*, withdrawn August 1963; No 6981 *Marbury Hall*, withdrawn March 1964 and No 4983 *Albert Hall*, withdrawn December 1963.
Revd Alan Newman

Second Edition

RAIL CENTRES:
BRISTOL

COLIN G. MAGGS

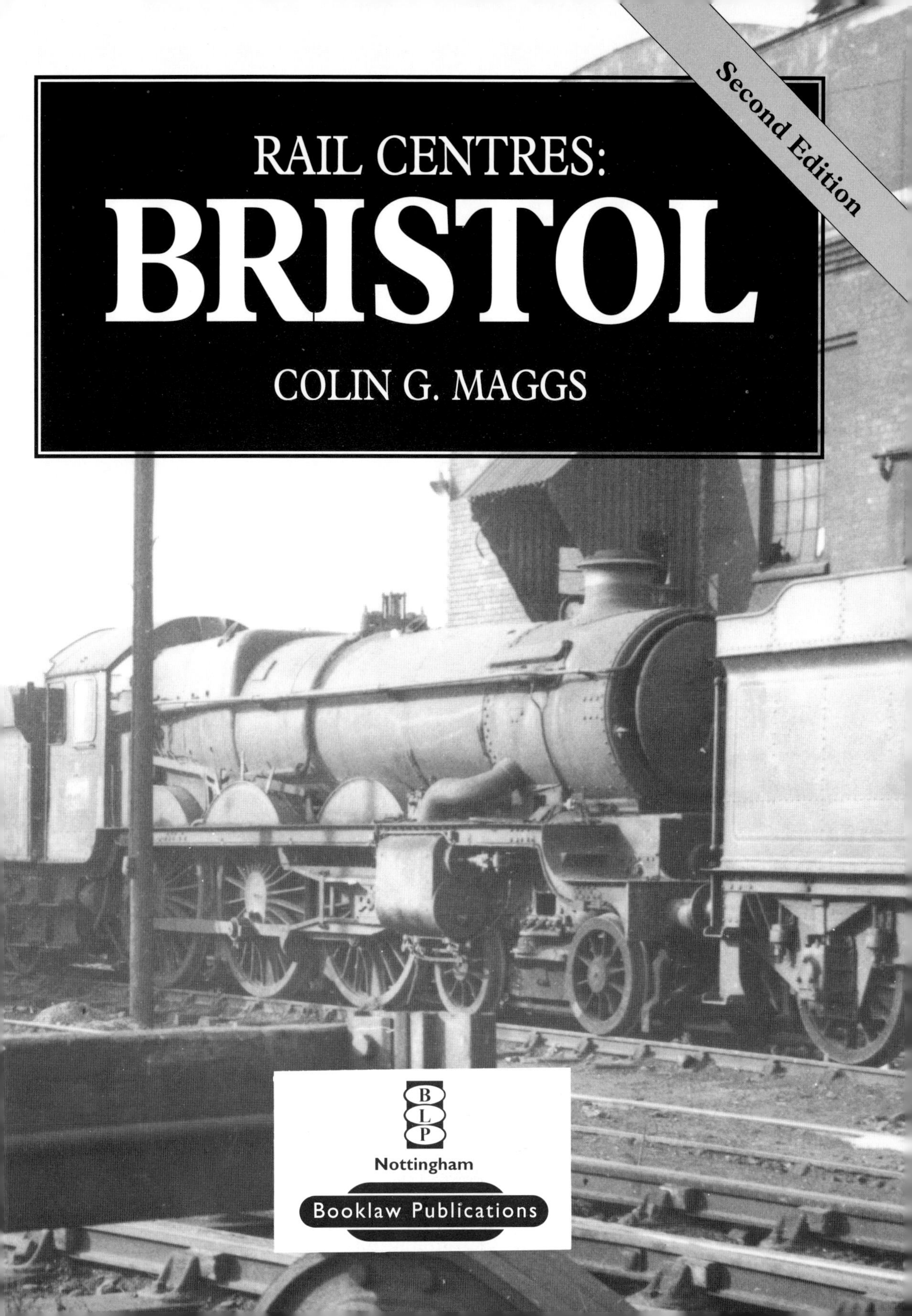

B L P
Nottingham
Booklaw Publications

First published 1981. Second edition 1996
by Ian Allan Ltd

This edition published 2008 by Booklaw Publications
382, Carlton Hill, Nottingham NG4 1JA

ISBN 1-901945-30-8

Printed by
The Amadeus Press, Cleckheaton, West Yorkshire

Acknowledgements
Grateful acknowledgement for assistance is due to: S. P. Anstey, M. J. Bishop; A. M. Child, J. Corin, Publicity Officer, Port of Bristol Authority; P. Davis, who gave great assistance on Bristol locomotive builders and who is writing a book on the subject; B. Edwards; A. Frost, Mrs J. Gaskell; E. S. Hancocks; E. J. M. Hayward; P. Smith; M. J. Tozer; J. W. P. Rowledge; D. R. Steggles and D. Wragg.

Right:
Contrasting front-ends at Temple Meads, 8 July 1983. Class 50 No 50044 *Exeter* and Class 33 No 33056 *The Burma Star* await departure. *Mike Ware*

Overleaf:
No W55032 at Ashley Hill with the 12.08 Severn Beach-Temple Meads, 30 March 1974. *P. J. Fowler*

CONTENTS

B132

OUTLINE HISTORY

There has been a settlement at Bristol for at least a thousand years. It developed at the confluence of the River Frome with the Bristol Avon at the lowest point that it was possible to bridge the latter and, indeed, the derivation of Bristol's name is from 'Brig-Stowe' meaning 'Bridge-town'. For centuries Bristolians earned their living by trading or manufacturing — the Bristol Merchant Venturers being famous — and until about 30 years ago, ocean-going vessels were able to moor at the city centre. So it is not surprising that, when railways were invented, they too converged on the city. As well as its size making it a centre in its own right, the shape of the Severn estuary makes Bristol the natural gateway to the West of England from the Midlands and the North, and the opening of the Severn Tunnel made Bristol the gateway to Wales from the south coast and the west.

It comes as a surprise to most people to learn that the Great Western Railway was not the first line to arrive in the city. In the latter half of the 18th century Bristol required coal for its developing industries. Although some came from collieries near the city, more was readily available at Coalpit Heath, nine miles to the north, and early in the 19th century several abortive schemes were put forward to link these collieries with Bristol. The Bristol & Gloucestershire Railway Act was passed on 19 June 1828. The northern half of the line was opened in July 1832 as this was shared by the Avon & Gloucestershire Railway which had the rest of its line complete. The 515yd-long Staple Hill Tunnel was eventually finished and the southern section of the BGR was ready for ceremonial opening on 6 August 1835. The horse-drawn wagons were fitted with temporary seats to carry shareholders and friends the nine miles to Coalpit Heath in three hours. The opening of the BGR reduced the price of coal at Bristol from 16 to 11 shillings per ton. Its Bristol terminus was at Avonside Wharf on the Floating Harbour opposite what was to become the site of Temple Meads station.

In 1839 the Bristol & Gloucester Railway, supported by the GWR — which had come into

Below:
Southeast view of Temple Meads *c*1842: departure entrance, left; arrival side, right. Disc and crossbar signal on far right. Flagstaff on water tower. A bus for Clifton is emerging with passengers off a Down train. Apart from the removal of the right-hand gateway, and the rather different road conditions, the scene is much the same today. *Engraving by J. Harris*

being four years previously — obtained an Act to absorb the Bristol & Gloucestershire. This Act also enabled the Bristol & Gloucester Railway (BGR) to extend the Gloucestershire line to Standish and lay a third rail over the broad gauge Cheltenham & Great Western Union Railway to Gloucester where it would link with the standard gauge Birmingham & Gloucester Railway. Although the doubling and extension of the BGR was prepared for the standard gauge, two years after the work started, Brunel urged the adoption of the broad gauge and the construction of a half-mile-long link from Lawrence Hill to the GWR near Temple Meads so that it could use the latter station. The BGR opened on 8 July 1844 completing a chain of rail communication from Newcastle-upon-Tyne to Exeter.

On 14 January 1845 an agreement was signed by the Bristol & Gloucester and Birmingham & Gloucester companies, both being worked as one until the Midland Railway took over on 7 May. The break of gauge at Gloucester proved a hindrance and an Act of 14 August 1848 allowed the MR to mix the gauge from Bristol to Standish and build an independent standard line between there and Gloucester. MR standard gauge trains first worked to Bristol on 29 May 1854.

The second railway to enter Bristol was the GWR. In the 1820s Bristol was the second city in the kingdom and it was not surprising that plans were put forward to link it with the capital. Early schemes foundered, but in the autumn of 1832 four Bristolians met in Temple Back, later covered by Temple Meads goods depot, and formed a committee which included representatives of the Society of Merchant Venturers and the Bristol & Gloucestershire Railway. This committee advertised for an engineer, and Isambard Kingdom Brunel was subsequently appointed. The Great Western Railway bill received Royal Assent on 31 August 1835.

The Bristol Board of Great Western directors, working independently of those in London, announced that the Bristol to Bath line would open on 31 August 1840. Just after 8am the 2-2-2 *Fire Ball* left with three first class and five second class coaches less than half an hour after the last rail had been laid. Some 5,880 passengers were carried on the first day in 10 trains each way and a revenue of £476 was taken, comparing very favourably with £226 when

Below:
Bridge over the Avon west of East Depot.
Engraving by J. C. Bourne

Right:
Rail routes to Bristol.

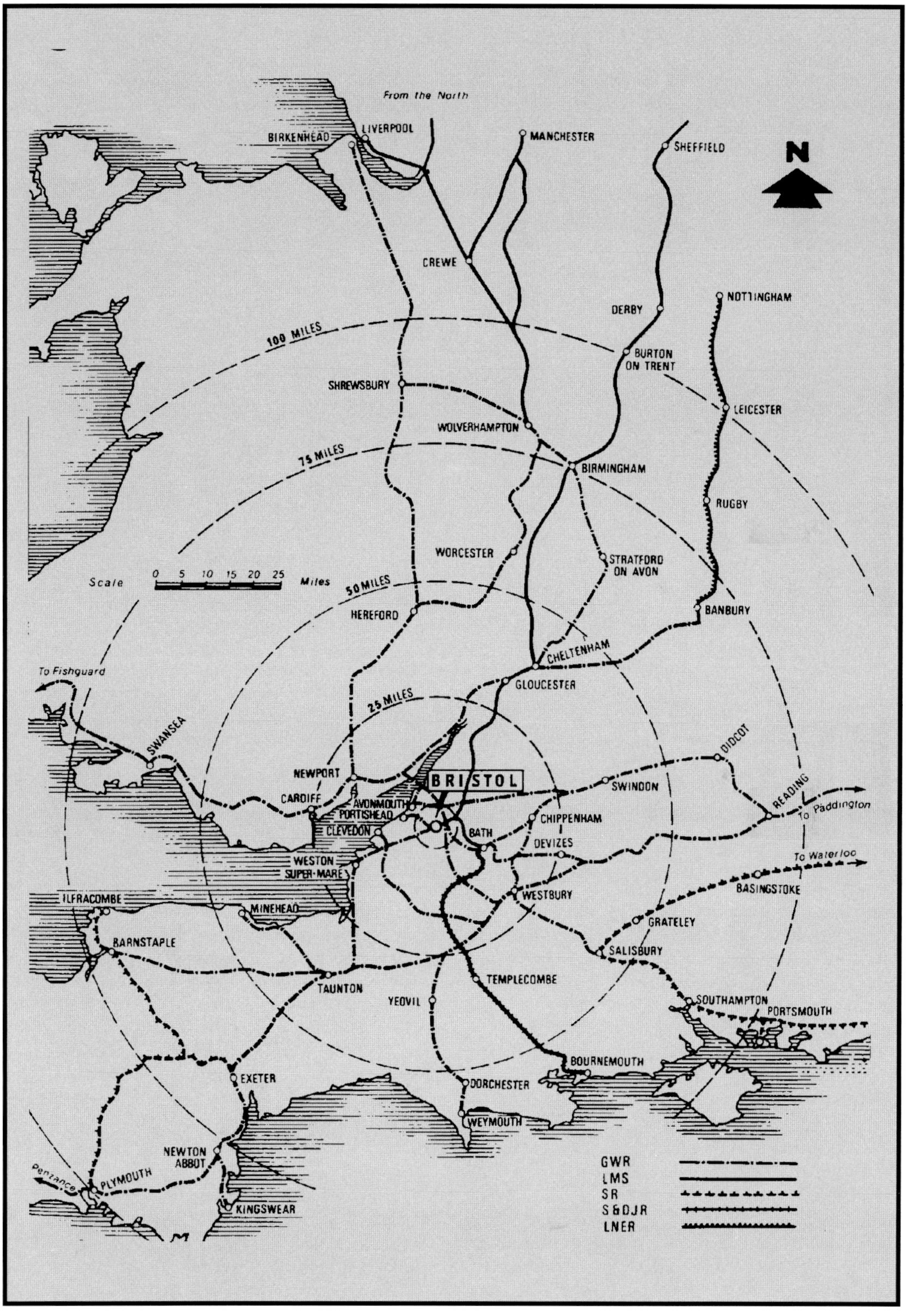
From the North
BIRKENHEAD
LIVERPOOL
MANCHESTER
SHEFFIELD
N
CREWE
DERBY
NOTTINGHAM
100 MILES
BURTON ON TRENT
SHREWSBURY
LEICESTER
WOLVERHAMPTON
75 MILES
BIRMINGHAM
RUGBY
WORCESTER
STRATFORD ON AVON
Scale 0 5 10 15 20 25 Miles
50 MILES
HEREFORD
BANBURY
CHELTENHAM
To Fishguard
GLOUCESTER
25 MILES
SWANSEA
DIDCOT
NEWPORT
BRISTOL
SWINDON
READING
To Paddington
CARDIFF
AVONMOUTH
PORTISHEAD
CHIPPENHAM
CLEVEDON
BATH
DEVIZES
WESTON SUPER-MARE
To Waterloo
BASINGSTOKE
ILFRACOMBE
MINEHEAD
WESTBURY
GRATELEY
BARNSTAPLE
SALISBURY
TAUNTON
TEMPLECOMBE
YEOVIL
SOUTHAMPTON
PORTSMOUTH
BOURNEMOUTH
EXETER
DORCHESTER
WEYMOUTH
NEWTON ABBOT
Penzance
PLYMOUTH
KINGSWEAR
GWR
LMS
SR
S&DJR
LNER

Above:
Interior of Brunel's train shed at Temple Meads *c*1845. On the right an Up train is almost ready to depart, while a Down train stands at the arrival platform, left. The centre roads are for spare rolling stock; notice men hand-shunting a wagon containing a brougham. Pillars supporting the roof are placed so close to the platform edge that some detraining passengers bump into them. *Engraving by J. C. Bourne*

the line was opened from Paddington to Maidenhead two years earlier.

The section through Box Tunnel being completed, the GWR was opened throughout from London to Bristol on 30 June 1841. The importance of the occasion was belittled by the *Bristol Mercury* which was so full of jubilation over the victory of the Liberal candidate in the General Election that it merely commented: 'Several trains passed over the line to and from London during the day. We have not heard of any accident occurring on the occasion, except that an engine which propelled the down train from town got off the rails near the station.'

A month after the GWR Act was passed in 1835, Bristol merchants issued a prospectus for an extension of the broad gauge to Exeter. Rapid progress was made. Within a month the estimated capital of £1.5 million had been subscribed, a survey completed and the necessary plans deposited. Of the 16 directors, 12 were Bristolians and none were directors of the GWR, though both companies shared the same engineer, Brunel. His assistant William Gravatt undertook much of the work.

Work began at the Bristol end of the line in February 1837, the chief engineering features being a 120ft masonry bridge across the New Cut and a deep cutting through the shoulder of Pylle Hill. In 1839 the plan for a temporary terminus at Pylle Hill was abandoned and it was decided to build a station adjoining that of the GWR. The B&E wished to save capital by not purchasing its own locomotives and rolling stock and in 1840 persuaded the GWR to lease the line to Bridgwater.

On 1 June 1841 thousands gathered at Bristol to see *Fire Ball*, once again selected to work an inaugural train, leave the B&E terminus with a train of eight coaches containing 400 passengers. The line opened to the public on 14 June when fares taken amounted to £302. The line was extended to Exeter on 1 May 1844 giving a main line 194 miles in length — the longest in the kingdom. The B&E was eventually absorbed by the GWR on 1 August 1876, a year after mixed gauge had been opened between Bristol and Taunton, mixed gauge (other than that of the Midland Railway), arriving at Bristol from the east in 1874.

The last of the main line railways to Bristol was the Bristol & South Wales Union Railway. As the crow flies, Bristol is only 25 miles from Cardiff, but just over a century ago the fastest way to travel between the two cities was to travel by rail via

Gloucester, a distance of no less than 93 miles! A short cut was obviously needed. The first attempt failed, as did the second which had the interesting proposal of a floating bridge across the Severn from New Passage. The third attempt, the Bristol & South Wales Union Railway, succeeded.

Parliament passed the necessary Act on 27 July 1857 granting powers for a railway between South Wales Junction, half a mile east of Temple Meads, and New Passage Pier where a ferry ran across two miles of water of Portskewett Pier, a short branch connecting with the South Wales Railway. Brunel was appointed engineer, though his health was failing by this time. He was succeeded by R. P. Brereton, with Charles Richardson as resident engineer. The $11^1/_2$ miles were constructed on the broad gauge. Richardson planned the piers so that trains could run to their ends and steamers land passengers at any state of the tide. It was while engaged on building these jetties that Richardson was led to consider the project of cutting a tunnel under the Severn.

Worked by the GWR, the BSWUR was opened ceremonially on 25 August 1863 and to the public on 8 September. It was Bristol's first suburban railway

Below:
Temple Meads in the 1860s: Brunel's train shed, right; Bristol & Exeter Railway offices, centre left; B&E terminus, left. Most of the tracks are mixed gauge. Several wagon turntables are provided to transfer stock to different roads. Two GWR horse boxes stand beyond the coaches. *Author's collection*

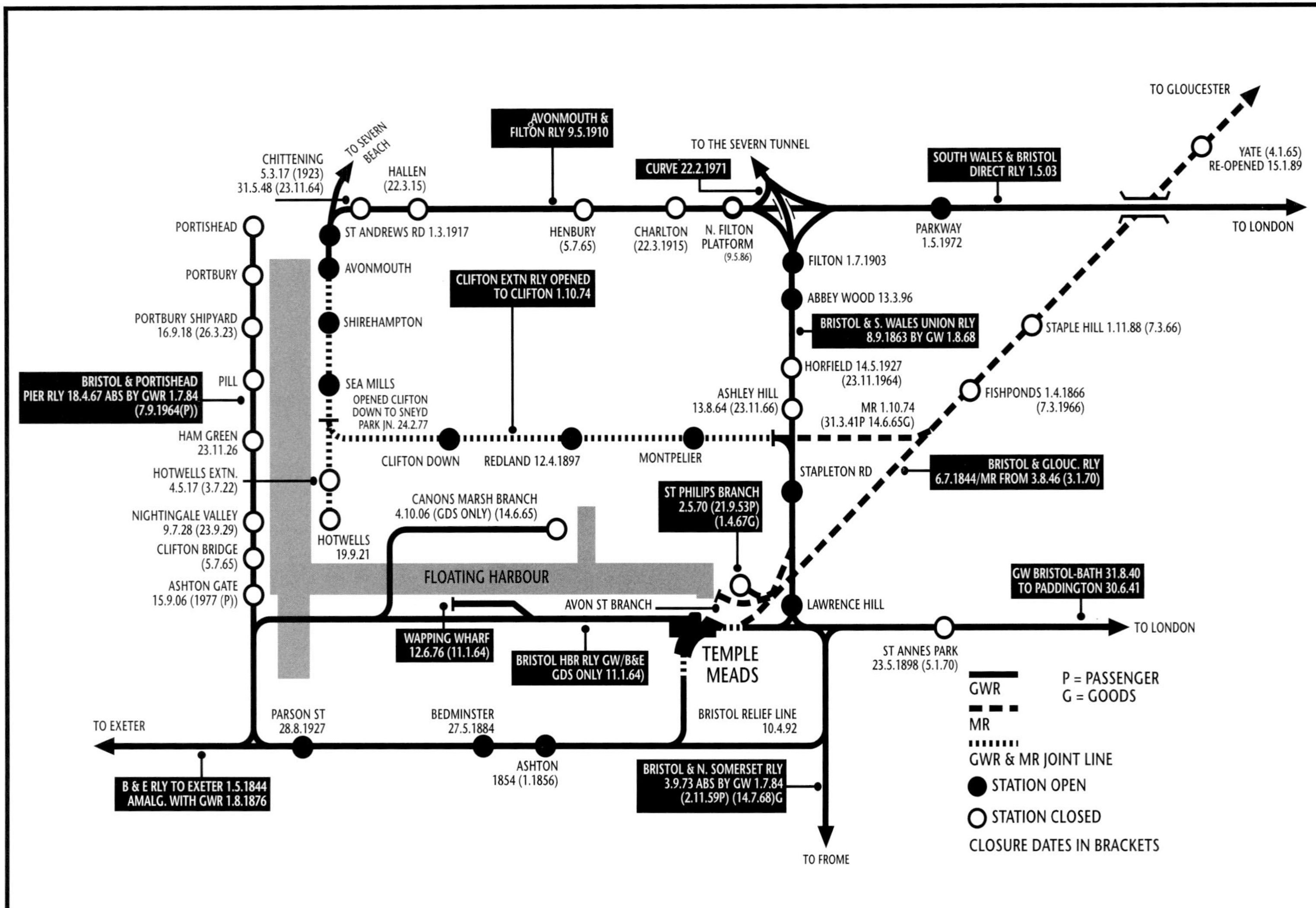
TO GLOUCESTER
YATE (4.1.65) RE-OPENED 15.1.89
TO LONDON
SOUTH WALES & BRISTOL DIRECT RLY 1.5.03
PARKWAY 1.5.1972
TO THE SEVERN TUNNEL
CURVE 22.2.1971
N. FILTON PLATFORM (9.5.86)
CHARLTON (22.3.1915)
HENBURY (5.7.65)
AVONMOUTH & FILTON RLY 9.5.1910
HALLEN (22.3.15)
TO SEVERN BEACH
CHITTENING 5.3.17 (1923) 31.5.48 (23.11.64)
ST ANDREWS RD 1.3.1917
AVONMOUTH
SHIREHAMPTON
SEA MILLS
OPENED CLIFTON DOWN TO SNEYD PARK JN. 24.2.77
CLIFTON EXTN RLY OPENED TO CLIFTON 1.10.74
CLIFTON DOWN
REDLAND 12.4.1897
MONTPELIER
FILTON 1.7.1903
ABBEY WOOD 13.3.96
BRISTOL & S. WALES UNION RLY 8.9.1863 BY GW 1.8.68
HORFIELD 14.5.1927 (23.11.1964)
ASHLEY HILL 13.8.64 (23.11.66)
MR 1.10.74 (31.3.41P 14.6.65G)
STAPLE HILL 1.11.88 (7.3.66)
FISHPONDS 1.4.1866 (7.3.1966)
BRISTOL & GLOUC. RLY 6.7.1844/MR FROM 3.8.46 (3.1.70)
STAPLETON RD
ST PHILIPS BRANCH 2.5.70 (21.9.53P) (1.4.67G)
LAWRENCE HILL
GW BRISTOL-BATH 31.8.40 TO PADDINGTON 30.6.41
TO LONDON
ST ANNES PARK 23.5.1898 (5.1.70)
PORTISHEAD
PORTBURY
PORTBURY SHIPYARD 16.9.18 (26.3.23)
PILL
BRISTOL & PORTISHEAD PIER RLY 18.4.67 ABS BY GWR 1.7.84 (7.9.1964(P))
HAM GREEN 23.11.26
HOTWELLS EXTN. 4.5.17 (3.7.22)
NIGHTINGALE VALLEY 9.7.28 (23.9.29)
CLIFTON BRIDGE (5.7.65)
ASHTON GATE 15.9.06 (1977 (P))
HOTWELLS 19.9.21
CANONS MARSH BRANCH 4.10.06 (GDS ONLY) (14.6.65)
FLOATING HARBOUR
AVON ST BRANCH
WAPPING WHARF 12.6.76 (11.1.64)
BRISTOL HBR RLY GW/B&E GDS ONLY 11.1.64
TEMPLE MEADS
BRISTOL RELIEF LINE 10.4.92
TO EXETER
PARSON ST 28.8.1927
BEDMINSTER 27.5.1884
ASHTON 1854 (1.1856)
B & E RLY TO EXETER 1.5.1844 AMALG. WITH GWR 1.8.1876
BRISTOL & N. SOMERSET RLY 3.9.73 ABS BY GW 1.7.84 (2.11.59P) (14.7.68)G
TO FROME
GWR
MR
GWR & MR JOINT LINE
STATION OPEN
STATION CLOSED
CLOSURE DATES IN BRACKETS
P = PASSENGER
G = GOODS

and had stations at Lawrence Hill, Stapleton Road and Filton. Ashley Hill was opened the following year and Horfield in 1927. There was a two-mile bank at 1 in 75 between Stapleton Road and Horfield. The BSWUR was converted to standard gauge on 7–9 August 1873. A total of 33 hours was allotted for the task, but it was completed within 28.

Although the opening of the BSWUR eased travel between South Wales and Bristol, it was far from ideal as the change from train to ship was inconvenient for passengers and not feasible for goods. The GWR proposed replacing the ferry by a $4^1/_2$-mile tunnel and on 18 March 1873 work started, a task fraught with difficulties and dangers. To cope with the expected increase of traffic on the BSWUR when the Severn Tunnel was opened, Narroways Hill Junction to Patchway was doubled by a new Up line being built. It was first used on 1 September 1886, the day the tunnel was opened to goods traffic. Passenger traffic began on 1 December, turning what

Left:
Diagrammatic representation of the railway history of Bristol.

Below:
Train emerging from the west portal of Bristol (or St Anne's) No 1 Tunnel *c*1845.
Engraving by J. C. Bourne

had been a branch into an important trunk route. To give a direct run from London to South Wales through the Severn Tunnel, in September 1886 an important 26-chain-long curve was opened from North Somerset Junction to Dr Day's Bridge Junction. From July 1887 main passenger services from London to South Wales were diverted from the Gloucester route to run via Bath and the new spur. The increase in the number of trains between Dr Day's Bridge Junction and Narroways Hill Junction, where Avonmouth trains diverged, led to quadrupling in November 1891.

Bristol was now an important rail centre, with main lines to London, Cardiff, Birmingham and Exeter. Added to this, all of the London–Exeter and London–South Wales traffic had to pass through the city until the opening of two cut-offs — the South Wales & Bristol Direct line on 1 May 1903 and the Castle Cary–Cogload Junction line on 11 June 1906.

Towards the end of the 19th century several Bristol to London schemes to compete with the GWR were proposed, but proved abortive. They involved running partly over the Bristol & North Somerset Railway or the Somerset & Dorset Joint Railway, to join the London & South Western Railway east of Salisbury.

The South Wales & Bristol Direct Railway was built as a result of people in South Wales being very dissatisfied with the GWR service and threatening to build an entirely new line from Cardiff to the LSWR east of Salisbury. The 31-mile long SWBDR built by the GWR to counter this threat had several advantages: it shortened the distance from London to South Wales by 10 miles and enabled the 1 in 75 incline to Horfield to be avoided; shortened the distance from London to Bristol by a mile; and relieved the busy Bristol–Bathampton line of London–South Wales traffic, this section not being easily quadrupled because of the heavy engineering works required.

The first through goods to use the SWBDR was on 1 May 1903 and the initial passenger train on 1 July. In contrast to the impressive ceremonies of the

Below:
Opening out Bristol No 1 Tunnel *c*1886 prior to widening the line. The wagon half-way up the cutting by the steam crane probably contains coal.
D. J. Hyde collection

Right:
View of Temple Meads looking Down *c*1905. Brunel's train shed, centre right; Wyatt's, centre left. Part of the goods depot is on the far right. *Author's collection*

Victorian era, the first train merely carried the Superintendent of the Bristol Division of the GWR and several other company officials. On 30 April 1933 the quadrupled tracks from Filton Junction–Stapleton Road were opened, two main tracks having been laid east of the original lines which became the relief lines.

The first of the branch lines, and the first line built as standard gauge radiating from Bristol, was the Bristol Port Railway & Pier. During the 19th century the size of vessels had increased to such an extent that some ships had too great a draught to navigate the Avon to Bristol safely. The BPRP and the Bristol Port & Channel Dock companies were formed in 1862 and 1864 respectively with almost identical promoters. On 17 July 1862 the BPRP received its Act to build a 5¾-mile-long single standard gauge line from a terminus at Hotwells to Avonmouth. As it was not proposed to cater for anything other than purely local traffic, no connection with any other railway was thought necessary. Benjamin Burleigh was appointed engineer. The precise opening date of 6 March 1865 was purposely withheld so that the line would not be overwhelmed by vast crowds that the single engine could not handle, and timetables were posted up outside Hotwells station only a few minutes before the departure of the first train. The BPRP, with virtually no goods traffic, realised that if it hoped to build a commercially viable dock at Avonmouth, through rail communication with other companies was essential. Since a line from Hotwells to Temple Meads across developed land would have been prohibitively expensive, a link was proposed from the BPRP at Sneyd Park to the BSWUR and the MR. As the financial position of the BPRP was too poor to attract investors, a separate company was floated.

The double track Clifton Extension Railway received its Act on 15 August 1867 and was managed by a committee formed of two representatives from each of the BPRP, GWR and MR, the last two companies providing the finance. The major engineering feature of the CER was Clifton Down Tunnel. Colonel Yolland's inspection train on 15 June 1874 was drawn by four locomotives — two GWR and two MR. The line opened for passenger traffic to Clifton Down on 1 October, all trains being well-patronised and pickpockets plying their trade on the crowded platforms. Beyond Clifton Down station work was still proceeding on the mile-long tunnel.

Above:
View *c*1910 from the footbridge showing the interior of Wyatt's train shed before the removal of the centre platforms in the 1935 alterations. In the centre, a Down Midland train is headed by a 2-4-0, with a GWR train on the left. *M. J. Tozer collection*

Right:
The four-road B&E carriage shed at Temple Meads *c*1925 set at right angles to the platform road, with part of the B&E offices seen on the right. Collett House now stands on the site of this carriage shed.
Author's collection

Although this part of the line was completed in May 1875, the Board of Trade inspector failed to pass Sneyd Park Junction to passenger traffic because he believed that the 150ft-long platform at Sea Mills station was inadequate for exchange purposes, though, in reality, few people would have required to change trains there.

With the opening of Avonmouth Docks on 24 February 1877, goods trains began working through the tunnel and the platform at Sea Mills was lengthened at the BPRP's expense. On 3 August 1878 Colonel Yolland sanctioned the opening of Clifton Down–Sneyd Park Junction to passenger trains, though in fact none ran because the GWR and MR felt that the BPRP line was not in a satisfactory condition to carry them. The Midland obtained parliamentary powers to install block signalling and charge the expense to the BPRP and eventually the line was opened to passengers on 1 September 1885. The single line beyond Sneyd Park was quite inadequate to cope with increasing traffic to and from Avonmouth, so Avonmouth Dock–Shirehampton was doubled on 16 May 1903 and Shirehampton–Sneyd Park Junction on 6 January 1907. After World War 1 Bristol Corporation decided to build a direct road to Avonmouth through the Avon Gorge to avoid the hilly route over the Downs. As there was insufficient room in the Gorge for both road and railway, it obtained an Act on 16 August 1920 to take over the line from Hotwells to Sneyd Park Junction, which closed on 3 July 1922. With the reduction in freight services, traffic was light enough to effect the economy of singling the line from Ashley Hill Junction to Avonmouth on 19 October 1970.

The first proposal for a line to Portishead was a colliery line in 1800, but this plan proved abortive. On 29 June 1863 the Bristol & Portishead Pier & Railway obtained parliamentary powers to build a line from the B&E at Bedminster to a pier at Portbury, with a minor

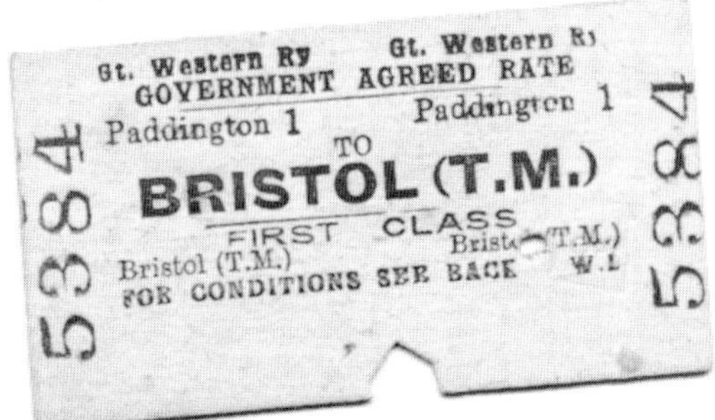

branch running to the village of Portishead. A change of plan caused the company to abandon the Portbury terminus and make Portishead the main line. The $9^1/_2$-mile single broad gauge branch was opened on 18 April 1867 and was worked by the B&E. The pier opened in June 1868 and was extended 300ft two years later so that vessels could use it at low water. The company was enterprising enough to operate steamers to Newport and Cardiff all the year round (the Severn Tunnel was not yet opened) and a special service to Ilfracombe in the summer with through rail and steamer bookings from the GWR and MR, passengers travelling to a special pier platform beyond the Town station.

In 1871 a bill was promoted to turn Portishead Pill into a dock. As the BPRP on the opposite bank also had dock plans before Parliament that year, both were competing for a subscription of £100,000 from Bristol Corporation. The GWR, as successors of the B&E, bought the railway and pier in 1884, the dock being sold to Bristol Corporation. The line had been converted to standard gauge between 24–27 January 1880. Portishead power station was enlarged after World War 2, the electricity authority taking over the site of the railway station. This necessitated the building of a new one in 1954 at a cost of £250,000 and it had the honour of being the first new station built since the war. The branch closed to passenger traffic on 7 September 1964 and to goods on 1 May 1967.

The first railway to reach Radstock was a branch of the broad gauge Wilts, Somerset & Weymouth Railway from Frome, which tapped lucrative coal traffic. Having thus projected a line into a mining area, it was thought profitable to continue it northwards to link with the main GWR line at Keynsham or Bristol, tapping further collieries *en route*. In 1862 plans for the Bristol & North Somerset Railway were drawn. The line was to run from Bristol, through Pensford to Radstock, and then climb over the Mendips on long gradients of 1 in 50, descending to Shepton Mallet and on to a junction near Bruton with the Somerset Central Railway. The SCR was one of the constituent companies of the Somerset & Dorset Railway whose Bath Extension had yet to be built. By an Act of 21 July 1863 the BNSR was incorporated to make railways connecting the MR, GWR and S&D, the backbone of the scheme being the standard gauge Bristol–Radstock line. Financial difficulties halted work begun in October 1863. The company's credit was not improved when its secretary, John Bingham, who had run up huge bills for legal and parliamentary expenses, was sentenced in June 1870 to 12 months'

GREAT WESTERN
RAILWAY
RECEIVING OFFICE
GREAT WESTERN RAILWAY
GOODS & PARCELS
RECEIVING OFFICE
TICKETS ISSUED HERE
G.W.R.
TICKET
OFFICE
GOODS & PARCELS
RECEIVED
VARSITY
J.B. HAMILTON
TUDENTS REVENGE ON SUFFRAGETTES HEADQUARTERS, BRISTOL.

imprisonment with hard labour for attempting to defraud W. M. Baillie, the company's Bristol banker and largest shareholder. Bingham had forged an endorsement on a draft of £536.

A new company was formed in the latter part of 1870, BNSR creditors receiving shares at par in lieu of their debts. A third contractor completed the railway and the GWR undertook to work the finished line which opened throughout on 3 September 1873 creating a break of gauge at Radstock until the Radstock–Frome branch was converted the following June. The GWR absorbed the BNSR on 1 July 1884, partly on economic grounds as the line tapping the coalfield had a considerable potential, while an additional factor for purchase was to prevent it from falling into the hands of the MR or LSWR. The branch closed to passengers on 2 November 1959 and following a landslip caused by a heavy storm, closed completely from Midsomer Norton to Marsh Junction on 14 July 1968.

When the direct line between Wootton Bassett and Patchway was opened in 1903, the need was felt for a straight route to and from Avonmouth Docks, so on 9 May 1910 a 6$^{3}/_{4}$-mile-long single line was opened from Filton and Stoke Gifford to Holesmouth Junction, Avonmouth, avoiding the heavily graded Clifton Extension line. The main feature of the Henbury line was the 302yd Charlton Tunnel. As well as being useful for goods traffic, the new route provided rail communication for villages north of Bristol until 30 April 1915 when the railmotor service was withdrawn and the halts closed.

Chittening Platform with its austere corrugated asbestos shelters was built during World War 1 to serve what would have been the second largest government factory in the country. By May 1917 the entire branch was doubled to cope with the expected traffic, but the entry of the USA into the war caused the British government to abandon the project.

After World War 2 the Bristol Aeroplane Co, Filton, developed the large 'Brabazon' airliner and between 13 October and 10 November 1947, temporary single line working was instituted between Henbury and Filton West to allow the installation of an aircraft level crossing over the railway in order to give access from the construction hangar to a new runway long enough to allow the aircraft to take off. When BAC wished to take aircraft over the crossing a telephone message was sent to Filton West signalbox and, if the line was clear, a release was

Above left:
The carriage approach to Temple Meads *c*1910. The gas lamp on the left is worth a second look. The tower's spire was destroyed by German raiders in World War 2. *M. J. Tozer collection*

Below left:
The GWR goods and parcels receiving office in Queen's Road with horse-drawn parcels delivery van outside, adjoining the suffragettes' headquarters which has been given a 'rough house' by students, 25 October 1913. *Author's collection*

Below:
Filton Abbey Wood to Frome opening ticket.

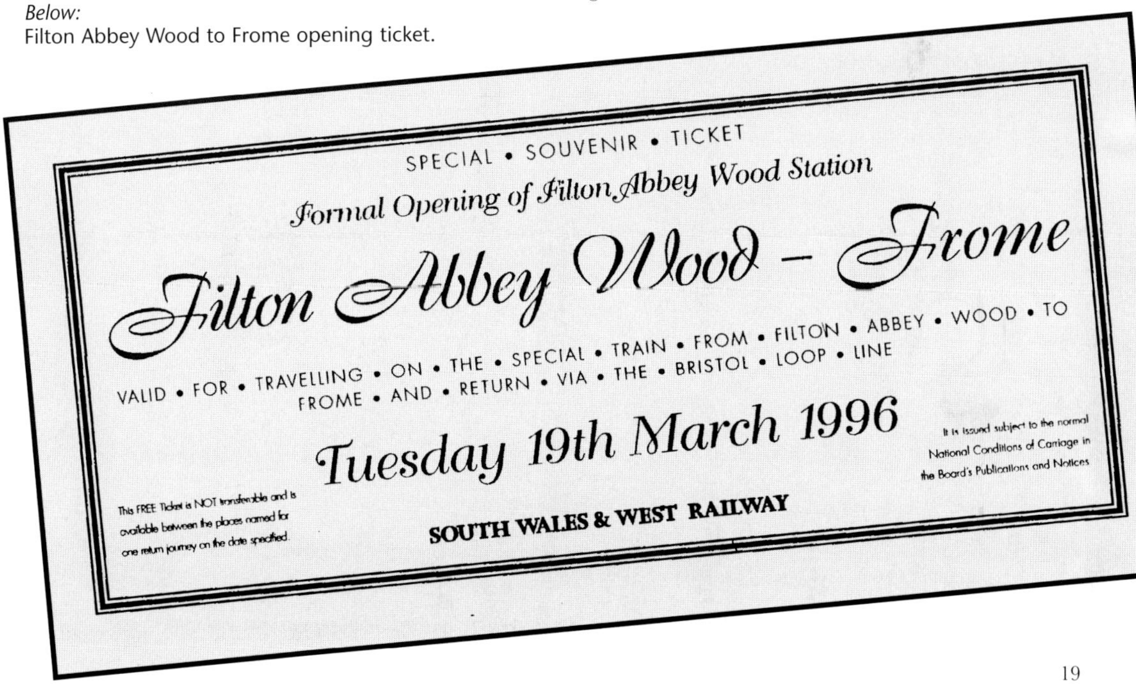

given to the motors operating the sliding gates. After the passage of an aircraft BAC restored the gates to normal and, when a proving circuit was made, train operation continued. Today the telephone is connected to the Bristol panel box.

The branch was closed to passenger traffic from 23 November 1964 and singled on 22 May 1966. During World War 1 earthworks were prepared for a curve from Filton West Junction to Patchway, but no track was laid. However, to facilitate traffic to and from South Wales, particularly zoo excursions to Clifton Down, the curve was opened on 22 February 1971. To cater for the merry-go-round coal trains from Avonmouth to Didcot and Aberthaw power stations, and liquid petroleum gas trains from Furzebrook to Hallen Marsh, the branch was doubled in the summer of 1992, temporarily reverting to single line when the Down road was used by stone trains for the second Severn crossing. This line is no longer signalled to passenger train standard.

To ease the situation at Temple Meads, which was becoming very crowded, an avoiding line from Pylle Hill through St Philip's Marsh to North Somerset Junction was opened on 10 April 1892. Due

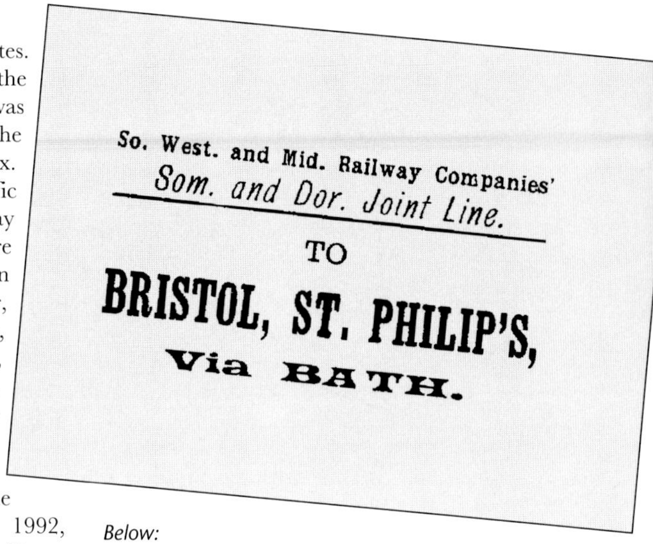
So. West. and Mid. Railway Companies'
Som. and Dor. Joint Line.
TO
BRISTOL, ST. PHILIP'S,
Via BATH.

Below:
A view of broad gauge 4-2-2 *Great Western* believed to be taken at Bristol. *LPC*

Right:
Map of the Bristol Area.

Below right:
Map of the Bristol Area – enlargement of the central area.

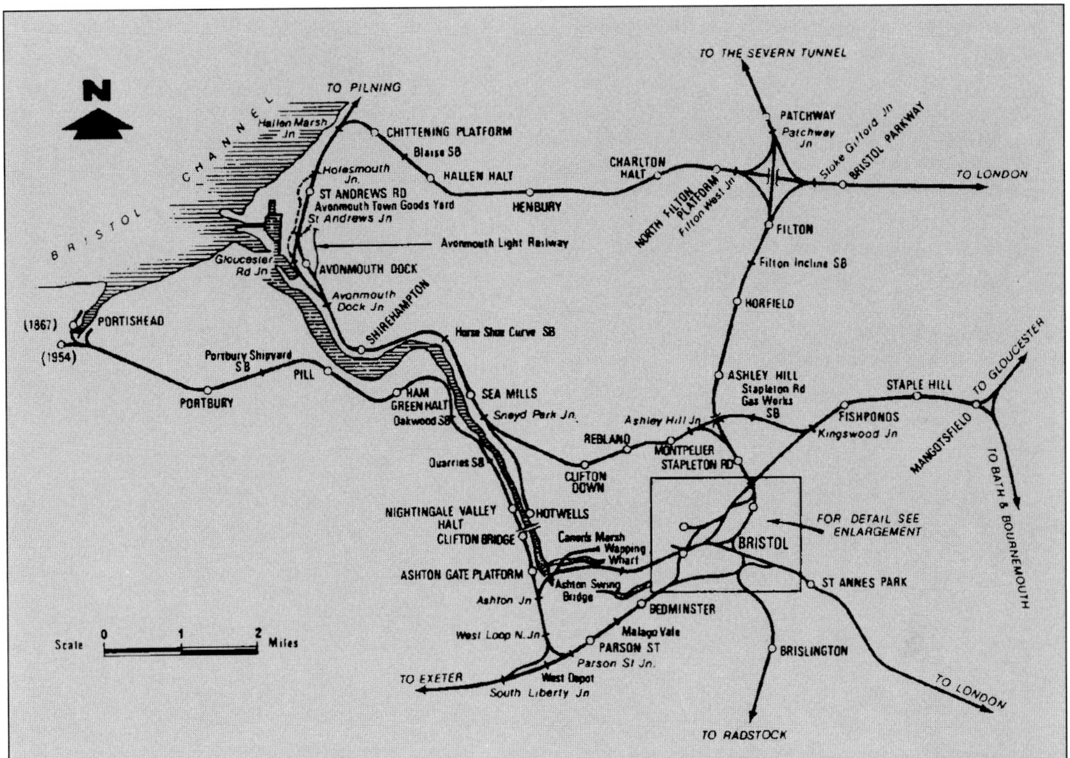

N
TO PILNING
TO THE SEVERN TUNNEL
BRISTOL CHANNEL
Hallen Marsh Jn
CHITTENING PLATFORM
Blaise SB
HALLEN HALT
Holesmouth Jn.
ST ANDREWS RD
Avonmouth Town Goods Yard
St Andrews Jn
HENBURY
CHARLTON HALT
NORTH FILTON PLATFORM
Filton West Jn
PATCHWAY
Patchway Jn
Stoke Gifford Jn
BRISTOL PARKWAY
TO LONDON
FILTON
Avonmouth Light Railway
Gloucester Rd Jn
AVONMOUTH DOCK
Avonmouth Dock Jn
Filton Incline SB
HORFIELD
SHIREHAMPTON
Horse Shoe Curve SB
(1867)
PORTISHEAD
(1954)
Portbury Shipyard SB
PILL
PORTBURY
HAM GREEN HALT
Oakwood SB
SEA MILLS
Sneyd Park Jn.
ASHLEY HILL
Stapleton Rd Gas Works SB
Ashley Hill Jn
STAPLE HILL
TO GLOUCESTER
FISHPONDS
Kingswood Jn
MANGOTSFIELD
TO BATH & BOURNEMOUTH
REDLAND
MONTPELIER
STAPLETON RD
Quarries SB
CLIFTON DOWN
NIGHTINGALE VALLEY HALT
HOTWELLS
FOR DETAIL SEE ENLARGEMENT
CLIFTON BRIDGE
Canerls Marsh
Wapping Wharf
BRISTOL
ASHTON GATE PLATFORM
Ashton Swing Bridge
ST ANNES PARK
Ashton Jn
BEDMINSTER
Scale 0 1 2 Miles
West Loop N. Jn
Malago Vale
PARSON ST
Parson St Jn.
BRISLINGTON
TO EXETER
West Depot
South Liberty Jn
TO LONDON
TO RADSTOCK

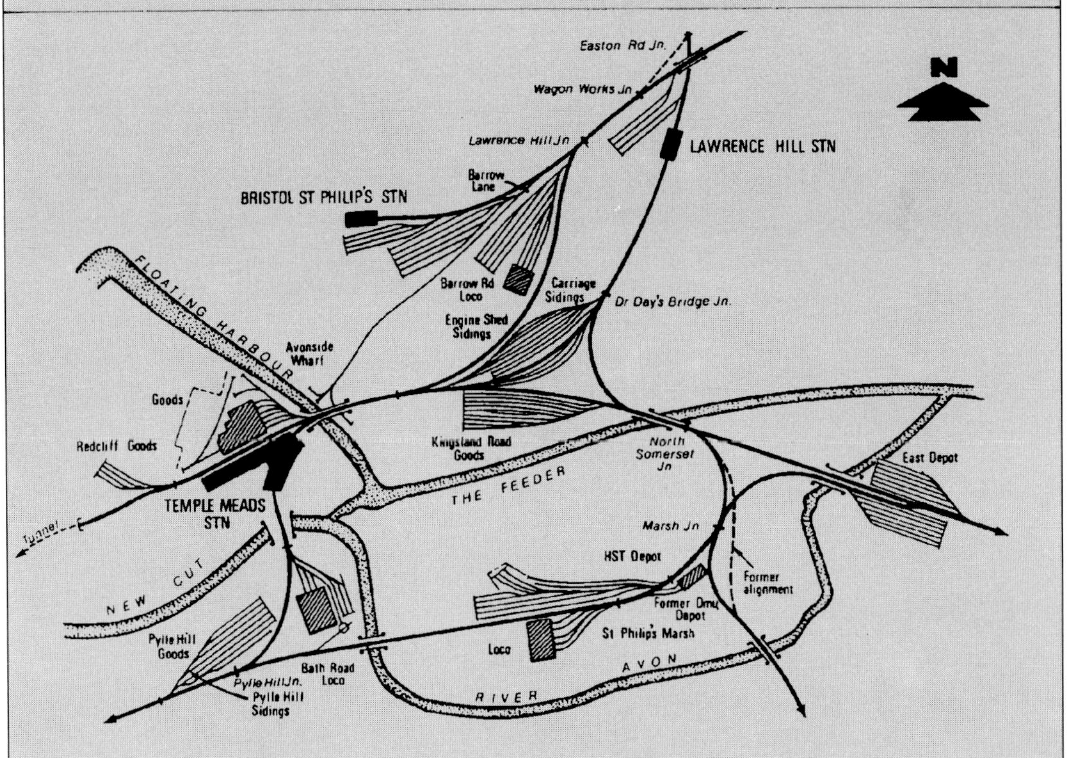

Easton Rd Jn.
N
Wagon Works Jn
Lawrence Hill Jn
LAWRENCE HILL STN
Barrow Lane
BRISTOL ST PHILIP'S STN
FLOATING HARBOUR
Barrow Rd Loco
Carriage Sidings
Dr Day's Bridge Jn.
Engine Shed Sidings
Avonside Wharf
Goods
Kingsland Road Goods
North Somerset Jn
Redcliff Goods
East Depot
THE FEEDER
TEMPLE MEADS STN
Tunnel
Marsh Jn
NEW CUT
HST Depot
Former alignment
Former Dmu Depot
St Philip's Marsh
Pylle Hill Goods
Loco
Bath Road Loco
AVON
Pylle Hill Jn.
Pylle Hill Sidings
RIVER

to decreased traffic, the western half was singled on 19 April 1970 and today is used only by empty coaching stock HSTs proceeding to or from the St Philip's Marsh depot.

Despite the curtailment of Britain's railway system, Bristol has remained an important rail centre because it is still an exchange point between main lines from London, South Wales, Portsmouth, Weymouth, the Midlands and the southwest, and in addition has a large hinterland which generates considerable traffic.

Above:
Bristol Port Railway & Pier 0-4-2T No 1, built in 1856 for the St Helen's Railway. Nothing is known of its history following its sale when the Clifton Extension Railway took over the line on 1 September 1890.
Author's collection

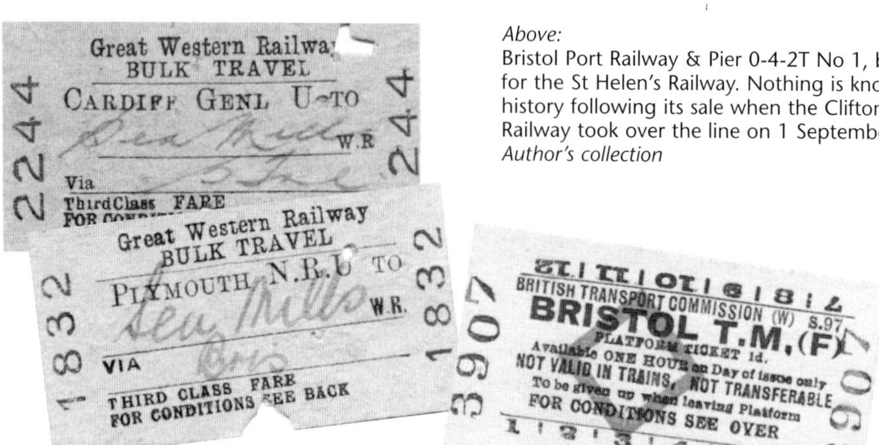

DEVELOPMENT OF PASSENGER WORKING

In 1840 the first service from Bristol to Bath offered 10 trains each way daily taking 25min for the $11\frac{3}{4}$ miles, including a stop at Keynsham. It ran in competition with 70 road coaches and soon put them off the highway. In December, when stations opened at Saltford and Twerton, an extra train was added each way, but third class traffic and goods were not carried until the opening of the line from London on 30 June 1841. The Down night mail was the fastest covering the $118\frac{1}{2}$ miles in 4hr 10min with 10 stops, but third class passengers travelling by goods train took $9\frac{1}{2}$hr. In 1845 the forerunner of the 'Flying Dutchman' ran to Bristol in three hours and on to Exeter in another two hours. In 1848 it was speeded to $2\frac{1}{2}$ hr to Bristol including the 10min refreshment stop at Swindon. The GWR was early in the excursion field and ran a trip from Bristol to London at 21 shillings — half the normal rate — on 29 September 1842, the train of 700–800 passengers being drawn by two engines. One interesting service from Temple Meads which only lasted for five months in 1864 involved slipping a coach at West London Junction for Kensington and Victoria.

A note in the early timetables stated that 'London time is kept at all stations on the railway, which is about 11 minutes before Bristol and Bath time, and 14 minutes before Bridgewater time'. Because of the inconvenience of local time being different from railway time, Greenwich time was adopted at Bristol on 14 September 1852, but only after a prolonged struggle on behalf of local custom. Bristol was one of the first cities to issue local railway guides. The Bristol Steam Packet and Railway Monthly Timetable and Family Calendar was published in January 1853 and followed in July 1854 by a rival publication wishing to cash in on its success.

Right:
No 5927 *Guild Hall* at Temple Meads with a 12-coach Birkenhead–Paignton train, 4 August 1934. *E. J. M. Hayward*

Below right:
No 5906 *Lawton Hall* leaving Temple Meads with a Manchester–Penzance train in 1934. The signalling has yet to be converted to colour lights.
E. J. M. Hayward

In view of the looming threat of the Bristol & London & South Western Junction Railway, in June 1882 GWR express fares were abolished and all trains except two expresses each way carried third class passengers. In April 1883, 11 through passenger trains ran to London compared with nine in 1862, while in July 1883 a new fast train left Bristol at 9.35am and reached Paddington in 2hr 50min, its Down counterpart departing at 6.20pm and arriving at Bristol in 2hr 55min. This train was a direct result of complaints of Bristol witnesses before the House of Commons Committee looking into the BLSWJR bill. In the spring of 1884 a sleeping car service was introduced for first class passengers.

The last public Up broad gauge train from Bristol was the mail which departed at 12.45am on 21 May 1892 hauled by 4-2-2 *Bulkeley*. Thirteen special trains taking broad gauge rolling stock from Devon and Cornwall passed through Bristol during the night *en route* for Swindon, while additionally some broad gauge coaches were placed in sidings at Exeter to be taken to Swindon later, as the mixed gauge east of Exeter was not immediately removed.

Following the abolition on 1 October 1895 of the compulsory refreshment stop at Swindon, the 'Cornishman' ran nonstop from Paddington to Bristol in 2¼hr, while on 28 July 1896 the longest nonstop run in the world was inaugurated when the first portion of the 'Cornishman' ran to Exeter in 3¾hr via the Bristol Avoiding line, while the same year restaurant cars were introduced for first class passengers. From 1 July 1903 the service was speeded by 15min, on which date 4-4-0 No 3433 *City of Bath* arrived at Temple Meads four minutes early. To

Above:
Two expresses at Temple Meads *c*1948 headed by No 6969 *Wraysbury Hall*, left and No 7014 *Caerhays Castle*, right. The latter has 'British Railways' on the tender in GWR-style lettering.
O. S. Nock/P. Q. Treloar collection

Left:
2-6-0 No 6381 heads a 14-coach west–north express up the 1 in 75 Horfield bank. A Pannier tank engine assists in the rear, 4 September 1936.
S. Miles Davey, courtesy P. G. Davey

Left:
No 6950 *Kingsthorpe Hall* at Narroways Hill Junction with an Up express.
W. H. Harbor/Author's collection

Below left:
No 4077 *Chepstow Castle* passes through Bedminster on 30 June 1962 with an Up express.
E. T. Gill/Revd Brian Arman collection

Below:
Excursion trips to away football matches, 1963/4.

mark the centenary of the Great Western Railway Act, on 9 September 1935 the 'Bristolian' was introduced, reaching Temple Meads in 1¾hr — 15min better than the previous best and giving an average speed of 67.6mph and 67.2mph in the Up direction. A 'King' was used for the first few months, but subsequently it was hauled by a 'Castle'. With the introduction of diesel-hydraulic 'Warships' in 1959 it was speeded to 1hr 40min, but for the winter of 1959 the Civil Engineer ensured that it was returned to the original timing of 1¾hr in order that 'Warships' could be limited to a maximum of 90mph. In 1961 when an even interval timetable was introduced, it called at Bath and to enable its loading to be increased to 10 or 11 coaches, the allowance was increased to 1hr 54min.

In 1960 the diesel-electric 'Bristol Pullman' was introduced, but its Swiss-designed Schlierer bogie failed to give the shorter British bodies a good ride. It left Temple Meads at 7.45am nonstop via Badminton; then returned at midday from London calling at Bath and finally ran the 4.55pm Paddington to Bristol nonstop via Badminton, the 110min being slower than the 'Bristolian'. From

ASSOCIATION FOOTBALL
1963/64 SEASON

Excursion bookings will be given in connection with Bristol City and Bristol Rovers away fixtures, forward and return by any train the same day. Special facilities will be advertised for F.A. Cup matches.

BRISTOL CITY

DATE	FIXTURE	STATION TO	FARE s. d.
Sat. 14 Sept.	Crewe Alex.	Crewe	32/6
,, 28 Sep.	Walsall	Walsall	25/0
,, 19 Oct.	Bournemouth	Bournemouth W.	16/9
,, 2 Nov.	Barnsley	Barnsley	42/0
,, 30 Nov.	Southend Utd.	Southend	35/0
,, 28 Dec.	Queens Park R.	Paddington	30/0
,, 4 Jan.	Colchester	Colchester	39/0
,, 11 Jan.	Notts County	Nottingham	33/6
,, 1 Feb.	Crystal Palace.	Paddington	30/0
,, 15 Feb.	Reading	Reading	20/0
,, 22 Feb.	Peterborough Utd.	Peterborough	45/0
,, 7 Mar.	Hull City	Hull	58/6(a)
,, 21 Mar.	Oldham	Oldham	41/0
Mon. 30 Mar.	Mansfield	Mansfield	37/6
Sat. 18 Apr.	Wrexham	Wrexham	35/0

a—Via Sheffield.

BRISTOL ROVERS

Sat. 7 Sep	Peterborough Utd.	Peterborough	45/0
,, 5 Oct	Millwall	Paddington	30/0
,, 12 Oct.	Brentford	Paddington	30/0
,, 26 Oct.	Crystal Palace	Paddington	30/0
,, 9 Nov.	Reading	Reading	20/0
,, 23 Nov.	Coventry	Coventry	25/0
,, 21 Dec.	Oldham	Oldham	41/0
,, 18 Jan.	Southend Utd.	Southend	35/0
,, 25 Jan	Notts County	Nottingham	33/6
,, 8 Feb.	Colchester	Colchester	39/0
,, 29 Feb.	Shrewsbury	Shrewsbury	27/6
,, 14 Mar	Walsall	Walsall	25/0
,, 28 Mar	Luton	Luton	34/0
,, 11 Apr.	Mansfield	Mansfield	37/6
,, 25 Apr.	Crewe Alex.	Crewe	32/6

TICKETS MAY BE OBTAINED IN ADVANCE FROM STATIONS AND AGENCIES.
FOR ENQUIRIES AT BRISTOL TEMPLE MEADS PLEASE RING BRISTOL 29-3451
Further information will be supplied on application to Stations, Agencies or to Mr. D. S. HART, Divisional Manager Transom House, Victoria Street, Bristol 1 (Telephone 2-1001, Extension 664).

Printed by THE SOMER PRESS Ltd., Midsomer Norton

SPECIAL CHEAP DAY RETURN FARES

Available any day by any train after 9 30 a.m.

(Where First Class accommodation is available, First Class Tickets are issued at approximately 50% above the Third Class fare.)

	Third Class s.	d.
From ASHLEY HILL		
to Bath Spa	2	1
Clevedon	2	9
Henbury	1	2
Oldfield Park	2	1
Severn Beach	1	8
Weston-super-Mare	3	3
From ASHTON GATE		
to Portishead	1	7*
From AVONMOUTH DOCK		
to Bristol (T.M.)	1	6
Clevedon	3	3
Clifton Down	1	0
Lawrence Hill	1	5
Montpelier	1	1
Redland	1	0
Sea Mills	0	7
Stapleton Road	1	5
Weston-super-Mare	3	9
From BATH SPA		
to Bristol (T.M.)	1	10
Clevedon	3	9
Keynsham & S.	1	4
Portishead	3	4
St. Anne's Park	1	8
Severn Beach	3	9
Weston-super-Mare	4	3
From BEDMINSTER		
to Bath Spa	2	0
Clevedon	2	3
Ham Green Halt	1	4*
Oldfield Park	1	11
Pill	1	4*
Portbury	1	7*
Portishead	1	9*
Severn Beach	2	3
Weston-super-Mare	3	0
Yatton	2	2
From BRISLINGTON		
to Clevedon	2	6
Weston-super-Mare	3	3
From BRISTOL (T.M.)		
to Avonmouth Dock	1	6
Bath Spa	1	10
Clevedon	2	4
Ham Green Halt	1	4*
Henbury	1	5
From BRISTOL (T.M.) *continued*		
to Keynsham & S.	0	10
Oldfield Park	1	9
Pill	1	5*
Portbury	1	8*
Portishead	1	10*
St. Andrew's Road	1	7
Saltford	1	4
Sea Mills	1	2
Severn Beach	2	1
Shirehampton	1	4
Weston-super-Mare	3	3
Yatton	2	2
From CLEVEDON		
to Bristol (T.M.)	2	4
Weston-super-Mare	1	9
From CLIFTON BRIDGE		
to Portishead	1	7*
From CLIFTON DOWN		
to Avonmouth Dock	1	0
Bath Spa	2	3
Clevedon	2	9
Oldfield Park	2	2
Portishead	2	6*
St. Andrew's Road	1	4
Sea Mills	0	6
Severn Beach	1	8
Shirehampton	0	10
Weston-super-Mare	3	3
From FILTON JUNC.		
to Bath Spa	2	4
Clevedon	2	10
Oldfield Park	2	3
Severn Beach	1	6
Weston-super-Mare	3	3
From FLAX BOURTON		
to Clevedon	1	8
Weston-super-Mare	2	6
From HAM GREEN HALT		
to Bedminster	1	4*
Bristol (T.M.)	1	4*
Parson Street	1	2*
From HENBURY		
to Ashley Hill	1	2
Bath Spa	2	8
Bristol (T.M.)	1	5
Clevedon	3	3
Horfield	1	0
Lawrence Hill	1	4
Oldfield Park	2	8
Severn Beach	1	2
Stapleton Road	1	4
Weston-super-Mare	4	1
From HORFIELD		
to Bath Spa	2	3
Clevedon	2	9
Henbury	1	0
Oldfield Park	2	3
Severn Beach	1	7
Weston-super-Mare	3	3
From KEYNSHAM & S.		
to Bath Spa	1	4
Bristol (T.M.)	0	10
Clevedon	3	3
Oldfield Park	1	2
Weston-super-Mare	4	3
From LAWRENCE HILL		
to Avonmouth Dock	1	5
Bath Spa	1	10
Clevedon	2	6
Ham Green Halt	1	7*
Henbury	1	4
Oldfield Park	1	9
Pill	1	7*
Portishead	2	0*
St. Andrew's Road	1	6
Severn Beach	2	0
Shirehampton	1	4
Weston-super-Mare	3	3
Yatton	2	6
From MONTPELIER		
to Avonmouth Dock	1	1
Bath Spa	2	1
Clevedon	2	8
Oldfield Park	2	1
Portishead	2	6*
St. Andrew's Road	1	4
From MONTPELIER— *continued*		
to Sea Mills	0	8
Severn Beach	1	9
Shirehampton	1	0
Weston-super-Mare	3	3
From NAILSEA		
to Clevedon	1	5
Weston-super-Mare	2	2
From NORTH FILTON		
to Severn Beach	1	6
Weston-super-Mare	3	[illegible]
From OLDFIELD PARK		
to Bristol (T.M.)	1	9
Clevedon	3	9
Keynsham & S.	1	2
Portishead	3	4
St. Anne's Park	1	8
Severn Beach	3	9
Weston-super-Mare	4	3
From PARSON STREET		
to Bath Spa	2	1
Clevedon	2	2
Ham Green Halt	1	2*
Oldfield Park	2	0
Pill	1	2*
Portbury	1	5*
Portishead	1	8*
Severn Beach	2	4
Weston-super-Mare	3	0
From PILL		
to Bedminster	1	4*
Bristol (T.M.)	1	5*
Parson Street	1	2*
From PORTBURY		
to Bedminster	1	7*
Bristol (T.M.)	1	8*
Parson Street	1	5*
From PORTISHEAD		
to Ashton Gate	1	7*
Bedminster	1	9*
Bristol (T.M.)	1	10*
Clifton Bridge	1	7*
Parson Street	1	8*
From PUXTON & WORLE		
to Bristol (T.M.)	3	0
Clevedon	1	5
From REDLAND		
to Avonmouth Dock	1	0
Bath Spa	2	2
Clevedon	2	8
Oldfield Park	2	2
Portishead	2	6*
St. Andrew's Road	1	4
Sea Mills	0	7
Severn Beach	1	9
Shirehampton	1	0
Weston-super-Mare	3	3
From ST. ANDREW'S ROAD		
to Bristol (T.M.)	1	7
Clevedon	3	3
Clifton Down	1	4
Lawrence Hill	1	6
Montpelier	1	4
Redland	1	4
Sea Mills	0	10
Stapleton Road	1	6
Weston-super-Mare	3	9
From ST. ANNE'S PARK		
to Bath Spa	1	8
Clevedon	2	7
Oldfield Park	1	8
Portishead	2	3*
Weston-super-Mare	3	3
From SALTFORD		
to Bristol (T.M.)	1	4
Clevedon	3	6
Weston-super-Mare	4	3
From SEA MILLS		
to Bristol (T.M.)	1	2
Clevedon	3	0
Clifton Down	0	6
Montpelier	0	8
Redland	0	7
Severn Beach	1	5
Weston-super-Mare	3	6
From SEVERN BEACH		
to Bristol (T.M.)	2	1
Clifton Down	1	8
Lawrence Hill	2	0
Montpelier	1	9
Redland	1	9
Stapleton Road	1	10
From SHIREHAMPTON		
to Bristol (T.M.)	1	4
Clevedon	3	3
Clifton Down	0	10
Lawrence Hill	1	4
Montpelier	1	0
Redland	1	0
Stapleton Road	1	4
Weston-super-Mare	3	6
From STAPLETON RD.		
to Avonmouth Dock	1	5
Bath Spa	1	10
Clevedon	2	7
Ham Green Halt	1	7*
Henbury	1	4
Oldfield Park	1	9
Pill	1	8*
Portishead	2	1*
St. Andrew's Road	1	6
Severn Beach	1	10
Shirehampton	1	4
Weston-super-Mare	3	3
Yatton	2	6
From WESTON MILTON HALT		
to Bristol (T.M.)	3	3
Clevedon	1	8
From WESTON-SUPER MARE		
to Bath Spa	4	3
Bristol (T.M.)	3	3
Clevedon	1	9
From YATTON		
to Bristol (T.M.)	2	2
Weston-super-Mare	1	6

* Available by any train throughout the day.

October 1960 it was re-routed morning and evening via Bath. In 1968 it was speeded to 100min including a stop at Bath, but decelerated by 5min in 1972 when a Chippenham stop was inserted into the Up morning and Down evening trip. The WR had three eight-car two-class units and the LMR two six-car one-class units used between St Pancras and Manchester until electrification. In March 1967 the two LMR units were modified for multiple-unit operation and two-class accommodation and placed in a 12-car formation for the Up run from Bristol and then divided for the midday return run, one to Bristol and one to Oxford, uniting again for the evening run from Paddington to Bristol. These midday services were poorly patronised and ceased in 1969. The introduction of the air-conditioned and better riding MkII coaches caused the 'Blue Pullmans' to have little appeal, so they were taken out of service in the spring of 1973.

Pre-production HST No 252001 ran various trains from Bristol at conventional speeds from 1975. HSTs were introduced on 4 October 1976, five each way knocking 22min off the time to Bristol Parkway and 15min off the time to Temple Meads. Four trains were in service, with one as standby and one for crew training. A full service of hourly trains from Bristol to Paddington began in the spring of 1977, the fastest covering the 118½ miles in 1hr 30min. As trains now

Above:
Cheap day return fares, 13 June–15 September 1955.

Left:
No 5085 *Evesham Abbey* at Temple Meads with the last Up steam-hauled 'Bristolian', 12 June 1959. No 4077 *Chepstow Castle* is on the left.
E. T. Gill/Revd Brian Arman collection

make at least three calls, the winter 1995-6 timetable shows that most Up trains take the fastest time of 1hr 35min and the fastest Down 1hr 36min, the majority taking 1hr 40min.

In May 1844 the opening Bristol–Exeter service consisted of seven daily each way and in July 1877 the first regular GWR standard gauge train ran through to Exeter. From July 1906 most Paddington–Exeter expresses were diverted from travelling via Bristol, to the new Castle Cary–Cogload Junction cut-off saving 20 miles and also helping to reduce pressure on Temple Meads. Thenceforward, for many years only one daytime train ran from Paddington to Exeter and beyond via Bristol, but recently three more have been introduced including one which runs via Bristol Parkway. In the summer of 1995 the 09.03 ran through from Temple Meads to Exmouth, but this was probably more for operating convenience rather than aiming to develop the service, as no through return train was provided.

The opening of the South Wales & Bristol Direct line on 1 July 1903 meant that trains for the Principality could avoid Bristol and four new direct expresses were run over the new line to South Wales. In 1927 two slip coaches for Bristol were detached at Stoke Gifford from South Wales expresses. The opening of Bristol Parkway in 1972 offered a quick route to and from Paddington; in 1995–6 the 'Red Dragon Pullman' ran nonstop in 75min. The opening of the Bristol Direct line offered three routes to London from Bristol: via Badminton, Chippenham or

Continued on page 33

Below:
No 5085 *Evesham Abbey* with the Up 'Bristolian' near Ashley Hill, 29 May 1959.
E. T. Gill/Revd Brian Arman collection

Bottom:
No 6014 *King Henry VII* with the Up 'Bristolian' near Ashley Hill, 15 June 1936.
S. Miles Davey, courtesy P. G. Davey

FOR YOUR PLEASURE

WEEKDAYS AND SUNDAYS

from

BRISTOL TEMPLE MEADS

to

WESTON-super-MARE

6/6

By any train

MYSTERY TRIPS

from

BRISTOL

SUNDAY 19 JUNE
SUNDAY 17 JULY
WEDNESDAY 10 AUGUST
SUNDAY 28 AUGUST

?

HOLIDAY EXPRESS

MONDAY	1 AUGUST —	WEYMOUTH
TUESDAY	2 AUGUST —	EXMOUTH
WEDNESDAY	3 AUGUST —	PORTSMOUTH
THURSDAY	4 AUGUST —	TORBAY
FRIDAY	5 AUGUST —	BOGNOR REGIS

75/-

Booking Stations

Bath Spa, Bedminster, Bristol (T.M.), Filton Jn., Keynsham, Lawrence Hill, Oldfield Park, Parson Street, Stapleton Road

HOLIDAY BARGAIN TICKETS

2 May to 30 September

From

BRISTOL T.M. & SUBURBAN STATIONS

To any 3 of the following destinations on Mondays to Fridays

WEYMOUTH	TORQUAY
EXMOUTH	PAIGNTON
BARRY ISLAND	PORTSMOUTH & S.
MINEHEAD	SOUTHAMPTON
EXETER	BOURNEMOUTH
DAWLISH	OXFORD
TEIGNMOUTH	

50/-

Out and back the same day—by any train

Opposite:
'Warship' class diesel-hydraulic D805 *Benbow* arriving at Temple Meads with the first diesel-hauled 'Bristolian', 14 July 1959.
E. T. Gill/Revd Brian Arman collection

Opposite below:
Advert of rail trips from Bristol, 1964.

Above left:
'Warship' class D821 *Greyhound* at Temple Meads with the 9.15am to Paddington on 18 July 1962. A diesel shunter stands in one of the centre roads and a Swindon three-car cross-country DMU will soon set off with the 9.10am to Cardiff General.
E. T. Gill/Revd Brian Arman collection

Left:
No 1009 *County of Carmarthen* at Temple Meads on 15 January 1961 with a train from Portsmouth. The headcode has been changed for ECS working to Malago Vale Sidings.
E. T. Gill/Revd Brian Arman collection

Below:
Two 4-4-0s meet near Ashley Down c1910. *Paul Strong collection*

Above:
No 4079 *Pendennis Castle* passing Malago Vale Carriage Sidings with a Down express, May 1958.
E. T. Gill/Revd Brian Arman collection

Left:
Steam railmotor and trailer, Ashley Down *c*1910. *M. J. Tozer collection*

Below:
'45xx' class 2-6-2T No 4551 at Temple Meads with a train to Frome, May 1956.
P. Q. Treloar collection

Above:
2-6-2T No 4595 storms up the 1 in 64 bank approaching Clifton Down Tunnel in March 1950 when single line track working was in operation to facilitate relining the tunnel.
R. J. Sellick/Author's collection

Left:
Auto trailer No 150 (ex-steam railmotor No 61) at Lawrence Hill leads an engine and another auto trailer *c*1933.
S. Miles Davey, courtesy P. G. Davey

Below left:
Green-liveried '55xx' class 2-6-2T No 5528 heads an Up stopping train at Temple Meads on 18 May 1957. *Revd Alan Newman*

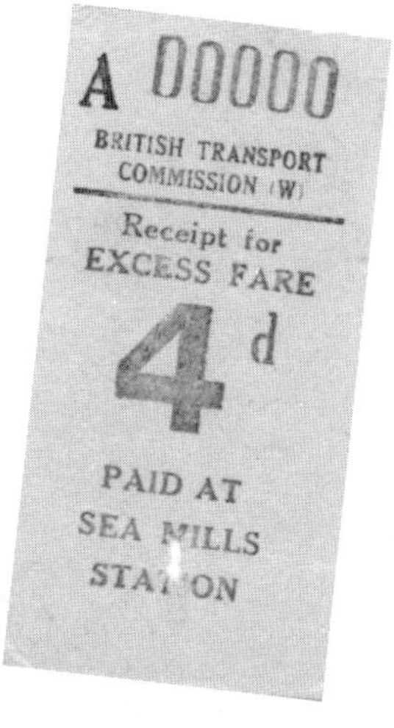
A 00000
BRITISH TRANSPORT COMMISSION (W)
Receipt for EXCESS FARE
4d
PAID AT SEA MILLS STATION

Right:
Railcars Nos 25 and 28 working the 2.30pm Temple Meads–Portishead near Portbury Shipyard signalbox, 5 September 1958. *Author*

Below right:
Ivatt Class 2 2-6-2T No 41208 pictured just beyond Portbury Shipyard signalbox working the 5.15pm Portishead–Bath Green Park–Bournemouth West on 5 September 1958. *Author*

Below:
Ex-LNER 'B1' class 4-6-0 No 61251 during the 1948 locomotive exchanges leaving Temple Meads with an express to Plymouth. *Author's collection*

Opposite:
Compound 4-4-0 No 936 near Kingswood Junction on 6 November 1936 with the 2.20pm Temple Meads–Bradford Forster Square. Notice the GWR Ocean Mails van behind the high-sided tender.
S. Miles Davey, courtesy P. G. Davey

Devizes. Although the Devizes line closed on 18 April 1966, reducing the number of routes to two, the opening of the Channel Tunnel revealed an opportunity to run services from South Wales through Bristol to Waterloo, again giving a choice of three routes to London from Temple Meads. In fact looking at them in detail there are now four routes as the Regional Railways Alphaline services run to Waterloo via Salisbury and Great Western Trains reach Waterloo via Reading, Acton and Kensington. Down trains from Waterloo are the fastest: Great Western Trains taking 1hr 50min and Regional Railways 2hr 20min. The best Eurostar service offers a time of 6hr 54min Temple Meads–Brussels Midi and 5hr 28min to Paris Nord. In preparation for through trains, engineers have assessed clearances on Platforms 3, 4, 7 and 8 at Temple Meads.

On 1 July 1908 an express was introduced from Penzance to Wolverhampton which ran through Bristol, and the following summer Bristol–Birkenhead and Weston-super-Mare–Wolverhampton expresses were added. That same year (1909) the GWR stirred things by retiming an Up express from the West Country to miss a connection with the MR 4.40pm to Birmingham by four minutes, but the GWR was not really competitive as the MR had a shorter mileage, easier gradients and fewer speed restrictions, while the GWR had no less than seven restrictions of 40mph or less. Between Yate and Standish GWR trains ran over the Midland line, that company limiting the GWR motive power to 'County' class 4-4-0 or de Glehn Atlantics, but in 1927 the restriction over Stonehouse Viaduct was relaxed to allow 'Saints' to travel over it at 30mph.

The Bristol–Gloucester service started with six trains each way, the fastest taking 65min. With the narrowing of the gauge in 1854, four through trains were run to Birmingham. On 6 August 1855 the MR ran excursion trains from Bristol taking 7,000 passengers to Birmingham at a return fare of 1s 6d for 177 miles. Following the opening of the Severn Tunnel in October 1888 the GWR threatened the MR's Scottish traffic from Bristol by putting on a train which left Bristol at 9.30am and connected with a West Coast express at Crewe. The MR made a countering move by initiating a 9.35am Bristol–Leeds

PULLMAN DIESEL EXPRESS SERVICES

High-speed luxury travel

THE SOUTH WALES PULLMAN

THE BIRMINGHAM PULLMAN

and

THE BRISTOL PULLMAN

Mondays to Fridays only

to connect with the Glasgow train at Normanton and the Edinburgh express at Leeds. It craftily avoided Birmingham so that passengers were not tempted to travel via the LNWR. Another disadvantage to the MR was that the GWR controlled bookings west of Bristol and therefore routed passengers through the Severn Tunnel.

1897 saw the introduction of dining cars between Bristol and Bradford, while two years later a completely new and lavishly equipped train was put on to woo passengers. By 1914 the best Derby–Bristol time had been reduced to 2hr 57min — 13min better than in 1900. Expresses called at Gloucester and Cheltenham, but in 1908 a nonstop was introduced between Bristol and Birmingham. From 17 July 1933 Compound 4-4-0s had to achieve a mile a minute average on the 10.25am and 2.25pm from Bristol, taking eight coaches over the 31.9 miles from Mangotsfield to Gloucester in 31min. On the first day of this working, Driver J. D. James of Bristol took No 1025 with 246 tons on the 10.25 to Gloucester in 31min 8sec and in the afternoon the train was hauled by Class 2 No 513. The prewar Up 'Devonian' was the fastest. It left Temple Meads at 12.35pm and, stopping at Gloucester and Cheltenham, reached New Street at 2.31pm. In the summer of 1956 it left

Above:
Cover of Pullman diesel leaflet, 1961.

Right:
Class 1P 0-4-4T No 1397 with a Clifton Down–Bournemouth West train just emerging from Montpelier Tunnel on 18 April 1936.
S. Miles Davey, courtesy P. G. Davey

Below right:
Driver of a DMU to Severn Beach collects a single line tablet from the signalman at Hallen Marsh, 25 July 1974. *Author*

Bristol at 12.30pm and arrived at New Street at 2.58pm, though the distance was a little longer as that year it had been re-routed via Filton instead of Mangotsfield. The 'Devonian', named from 1927, was a misnomer for half the year because in the winter service the Devonian composition shrank to three coaches between Bradford and Paignton. Northbound as far as Bristol these were attached to a west to north express (8.45am Plymouth–Crewe) and westbound to the 3.50pm Bristol, an originating train. About 1937 the introduction of 'Jubilees' allowed 83min to be saved between Leeds and Bristol, and 53min Nottingham–Bristol. For the summer of 1952 the 'Cornishman' ran from Wolverhampton and Birmingham to Penzance.

Continued on page 38

Above:
Class 5 4-6-0 No 45040 enters Temple Meads with a Bradford–Paignton express, 26 June 1949. A '45xx' 2-6-2T is to its right. *Pursey Short*

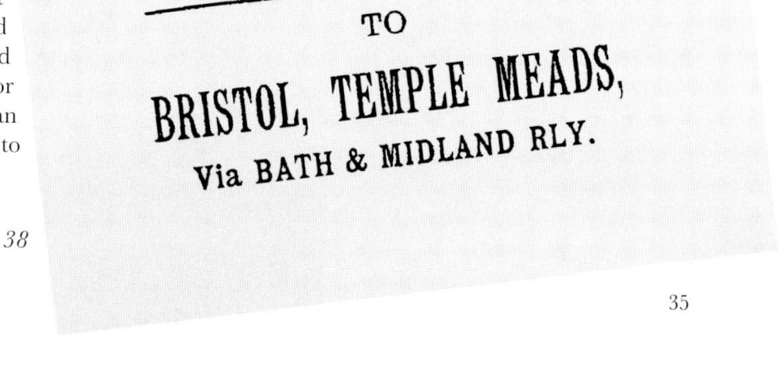

Above:
Up 'Bristol Pullman' passes St Anne's Park, 29 May 1963. The cutting in the background used to be Bristol No 1 Tunnel.
E. T. Gill/Revd Brian Arman collection

Right:
'Star' class 4-6-0 No 4062 *Malmesbury Abbey* at Temple Meads, 1951. The fireman has just thrown the water crane bag out of the tender tank and is about to close the tank's lid.
W. H. Harbor/Author's collection

Below right:
33034 arrives at Temple Meads with the 08.30 Brighton–Cardiff. A Class 47 to complete the rest of the run waits on the left, 4 September 1986. *Author*

Opposite above:
43093 at Temple Meads with the 07.20 Penzance–Edinburgh, the 'Cornish Scot', on 31 October 1995. The Royal Mail sorting office conveyor is in the bridge above the power car. *Author*

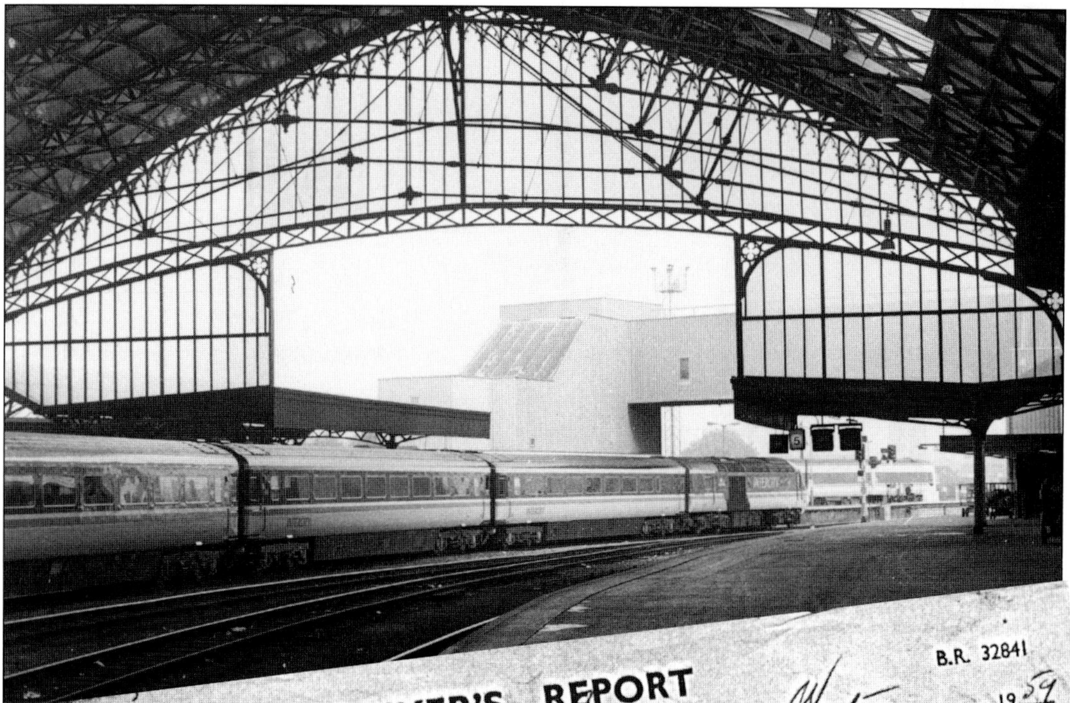

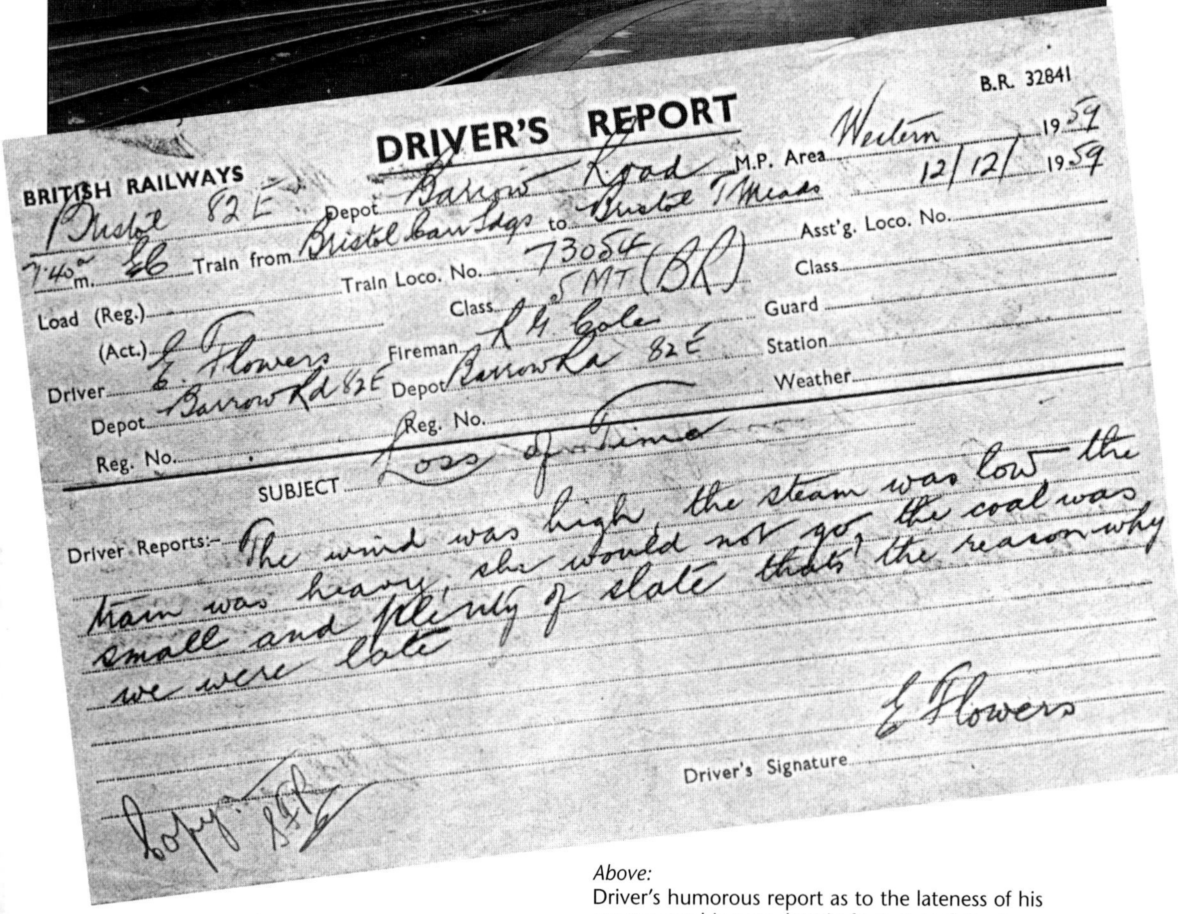

B.R. 32841

BRITISH RAILWAYS

DRIVER'S REPORT

M.P. Area Western 19 59

12/12/ 1959

Bristol 82E Depot Barrow Road

7.40 a.m. EC Train from Bristol Carr Sdgs to Bristol T Meads

Asst'g. Loco. No.

Train Loco. No. 73054

Class

Load (Reg.)

Class 5MT (BR)

Guard

(Act.)

Fireman L G Cole

Station

Driver E Flowers

Depot Barrow Rd 82E

Weather

Depot Barrow Rd 82E

Reg. No.

Reg. No.

SUBJECT Loss of Time

Driver Reports:- The wind was high the steam was low the train was heavy, she would not go, the coal was small and plenty of slate that's the reason why we were late

E Flowers

Driver's Signature

Copy

Above:
Driver's humorous report as to the lateness of his empty coaching stock train from Bristol Carriage Sidings to Temple Meads, 12 December 1959.

Today Bristol is served by 17 trains from Birmingham, the 'Cornishman' running the $89\frac{1}{2}$ miles from New Street to Temple Meads in 81min. The north of England and Scotland are connected by a good service of through named trains:

The 'Armada':	Plymouth–Newcastle
The 'Devon Scot':	Plymouth–Aberdeen
The 'Devonian':	Paignton–Newcastle
The 'Cornish Scot':	Penzance–Edinburgh
The 'Cornishman':	Penzance–Edinburgh.

The opening of Yate station on 11 May 1989 and Cam & Dursley 18 May 1994 means that now eight stopping trains run between Bristol and Gloucester.

In the days of the New Passage to Portskewett ferry, the service from Bristol to South Wales was unreliable as it depended on weather and tides, steamers sometimes being unable to leave the piers and sometimes not able to land. When Portskewett Pier was destroyed by fire on 23 May 1881, passengers were conveyed throughout by rail to South Wales via the MR, across the Severn Bridge to Lydney and down the South Wales line. This route took $2\frac{1}{4}$hr, or 25min less than the more direct ferry, but lasted only until 15 June when temporary repairs made the pier available once more. The Severn Tunnel was used for local traffic from 1 December 1886 saving 75min on the journey from Bristol to Cardiff. It was first used by London to South Wales passenger trains on 1 July 1887, trains travelling via Bristol and adding to the congestion there as the Badminton cut-off had yet to be built. To avoid turning the engine at Temple Meads, Cardiff-Portsmouth trains made Stapleton Road their main Bristol station, though with the DMUs of today they have reverted to reversal at Temple Meads in order to simplify connections with other trains.

Motive power has shown a considerable variety, 'Hymeks' beginning in the summer of 1961, four years later changing to InterCity DMUs to ease reversal at Temple Meads. The introduction of a regular two-hourly interval Bristol–Portsmouth service saw the appearance of SR '3H' units and as a

Above:
No 37602 in St Philip's Marsh depot with EPS (European Passenger Services) logo, 16 January 1996.
Author

result of the growth of patronage, a revised service from 1 July 1974 used either '3H' or cross-country units in six-car formation. During late September 1976 many Eastleigh-based '3H' DEMUs were taken out of service and Class 33 locomotives hauled rakes of '4TC' units on '3H' diagrams. A revised service in May 1977 saw Portsmouth trains hauled by Class 31s which in May 1980 were replaced by Class 33s. In turn these were displaced by Sprinters in 1988 and Super Sprinters in 1991. In the winter of 1995–6 35 trains ran from Temple Meads to South Wales, most of these being Regional Railways Alphaline services. Regional Railways run a train from Bristol to Maesteg for operational reasons, while an interesting cross-country working is the 13.38 Newcastle–Swansea, which after calling at Bristol Parkway, deviates to Temple Meads *en route* to South Wales thus retracing its route back to Filton. The 07.15 Swansea–York is a similar working. A remarkably good service of late evening trains is provided from Temple Meads to Cardiff departing at 21.27, 21.48 and 21.59.

Because of gradients of 1 in 60, the four daily trains from Bristol to Radstock took an hour for the 16 miles. In 1913 nine Down passenger trains ran daily over the BNSR from Bristol, two of these originating from Portishead, one from Weston-super-Mare and another from Wells. Of the eight Up, two came from Wells and Portishead. The service was well maintained after Nationalisation, including the 5.55pm Frome fast. Carrying express headlights and calling only at Radstock and Pensford, it made a connection between the Up Channel Islands boat train and the North Mail from Bristol. With a decline in the number of passengers, the service over the branch was halved in September 1958 and totally withdrawn just over a year later. In the 1930s the line was used by Saturdays-only summer expresses from Birmingham to Weymouth.

Right:
Pacer No 143612 leaves Platform 5 Temple Meads with the 11.00 Weston-super-Mare–Gloucester on 31 October 1995. The 'Cornish Scot', 07.20 Penzance–Edinburgh, is on the right. *Author*

Below:
Transrail No 37411 at Temple Meads with the 08.40 Weymouth–Temple Meads, 31 October 1995. *Author*

TRAIN SERVICE between CLIFTON DOWN and WESTON-SUPER-MARE.

WEEK DAYS. (DOWN)

DOWN.	Mi. 1 2 a.m	1 2 3 a.m.	T 1 2 P a.m	1 2 3 a.m.	1 2 P a.m.	1 2 3 a.m	1 2 3 a.m	1 2 3 a.m	T 1 2 3 a.m	T 1 2 3 a.m	Fast 1 2 p.m	1 2 3 p.m
Clifton Down	..	6 55	..	..	..	8 35	9 30	..	10 25	11 25	..	..
Montpellier	..	6 58	..	..	..	8 38	9 33	..	10 28	11 28	..	..
Stapleton Road	..	7 3	..	..	..	8 43	9 38	..	10 33	11 33	..	..
Lawrence Hill	..	7 8	..	..	..	8 48	9 43	..	10 38	11 38	..	..
Bristol arr	..	7 15	..	..	..	8 55	9 50	..	10 45	11 45	..	..
Bristol dep	5 15	7 20	7 30	8 5	8 25	9 15	—	10 50	11 0	11 50	12 20	12 40
Bedminster	..	..	7 35	..	8 30	..	..	..	11 5	..	..	..
Bourton	..	..	7 49	..	8 42	..	..	..	11 16	..	..	..
Nailsea	..	..	7 58	..	8 52	..	..	..	11 25	..	..	..
Yatton	..	7 40	8 12	8 25	9 2	9 38	..	11 15	11 36	12 14	..	1 5
Clevedon dp	..	..	7 55	..	8 45	9 25	..	10 55	10 55	12 0	..	12 0
Clevedon ar.	..	..	8 25	..	9 15	9 50	..	11 30	..	..	..	..
Worle	..	..	8 22	..	9 12	..	..	..	11 46	..	..	1 18
Weston Junction	5 43	7 57	8 31	..	9 22	9 49	..	11 30	11 56	12 33	12 48	1 19
Weston-s-Mare	5 58	8 5	9 10	..	9 28	10 0	..	11 40	12 8	12 35	1 0	1 34

DOWN.	1 2 3 p.m	1 2 3 p.m.	1 2 3 p.m	1 2 3 p.m	T 1 2 3 p.m	1 2 3 p.m	1 2 3 p.m	Fast 1 2 p.m	T 1 2 3 p.m	1 2 3 p.m	
Clifton Down	12 40	..	2 20	3 30	4 45	5 35	..	6 30	8 20	8 45	..
Montpellier	12 43	..	2 23	3 33	4 48	5 38	..	6 33	8 23	8 48	..
Stapleton Road	12 48	..	2 28	3 38	4 53	5 43	..	6 38	8 28	8 53	..
Lawrence Hill	12 53	..	2 33	3 43	4 58	5 48	..	6 43	8 33	8 58	..
Bristol arr	1 0	..	2 40	3 50	5 5	5 55	..	6 50	8 40	9 5	..
Bristol dep	1 40	3 0	3 15	4 40	5 15	6 0	..	8 15	8 50	—	..
Bedminster	1 45	..	1 2 Cla.	4 45	..	6 5	..	..	8 55	..	..
Bourton	1 54	..		4 56	..	6 19	..	..	9 3	..	..
Nailsea	2 3	..	3 35	5 4	..	6 27	..	..	9 10	..	..
Yatton	2 14	3 24	3 47	5 14	S	6 39	..	..	9 20	..	..
Clevedon dp	..	3 10	3 10	..	..	6 22	..	..	9 5	..	..
Clevedon ar.	2 26	3 36	4 15	5 25	5 50	6 55	..	..	9 45	..	..
Worle	..	..	4 3	..	..	6 48	..	..	9 28	..	..
Weston Junction	..	3 45	4 11	..	5 44	7 0	..	..	9 38	..	..
Weston-s-Mare	..	3 50	4 21	..	5 50	7 10	..	8 50	9 45	..	..

SUNDAYS. (DOWN) and FARES from CLIFTON DOWN.

DOWN.	1 2 P a.m	1 2 P p.m	1 2 3 p.m	1 2 3 p.m	1 2 3 p.m	1 3 3 p.m	1	2	3	Par	1 Ret.	2 Ret.
Clifton Down	..	2 30	4 0	5 30	6 30	8 15	..	..	..	..	..	..
Montpellier	..	2 33	4 3	5 33	6 33	8 18	0/3	0/2	0/1	0/1	0/5	[illegible]
Stapleton Road	..	2 38	4 8	5 38	6 38	8 23	0/6	0/4	0/3	0/2	0/9	[illegible]
Lawrence Hill	..	2 43	4 13	5 43	6 43	8 28	0/6	0/4	0/3	0/2½	0/9	[illegible]
Bristol arr	..	2 50	4 20	5 50	6 50	8 35	0/6	0/4	0/3	0/3	0/9	[illegible]
Bristol dep	6 30	3 30	1 2 3	—	—	—	..	..	..	..	..	..
Bedminster	..	..		..	..	..	..	..	..	..	..	..
Bourton	..	..		..	..	..	1/8	1/3	0/7½	0/7½	[illegible]	[illegible]
Nailsea	6 48	3 48		..	..	..	2/2	1/8	0/10	0/10	3/1	[illegible]
Yatton	6 59	3 59		..	..	..	3/0	2/4	1/2	1/2	4/3	3/1
Clevedon dp	6 47	3 45		..	..	..	3/0	2/4	1/6	1/6	4/3	3/1
Clevedon ar.	7 10	4 15		..	..	..						
Worle	7 8	4 8		..	..	..	3/9	2/11	1/5½	1/5½	4/9	3/6
Weston Junction	7 17	4 17		..	..	..	..	..	..	..	..	..
Weston-s-Mare	7 27	4 30		..	..	..	4/3	3/4	1/10	1/10	5/9	4/2

WEEK DAYS. (UP)

UP.	1 2 3 a.m.	M 1 2 P a.m.	1 2 3 a.m.	T 1 2 3 a.m.	1 2 P a.m.	M 1 2 P a.m.	T 1 2 3 a.m.	1 2 a.m.	1 2 P p.m.	1 2 p.m.	
Weston-s-Mare dep	..	6 40	..	8 40	..	8 20	10 0	10 40	..	12 11	..
Weston Junction	..	6 48	..	..	..	8 55	10 5	10 55	..	12 26	..
Worle	..	6 55	..	..	..	9 8	..	..	..	..	..
Yatton	..	7 6	..	..	9 0	9 13	10 17	11 10	12 12	..	..
Clevedon dep.	..	6 50	..	..	8 45	8 45	10 3	10 55	12 0	..	..
Clevedon arr.	..	7 18	..	..	..	9 50	10 30	11 30	..	..	..
Nailsea	..	7 14	..	..	9 10	9 21	..	11 23	12 22	..	..
Bourton	..	7 21	..	..	9 18	9 30	..	..	12 30	..	..
Bedminster	..	7 32	..	9 16	9 31	9 46	10 37	11 41	12 42	1 2	..
Bristol arr.	..	7 35	..	9 20	9 35	9 50	10 40	11 45	12 45	1 5	..
Bristol dep.	6 30	8 5	9 5	9 25	—	—	10 50	12 15	1 2 3	—	..
Lawrence Hill	..	8 10	9 10	..	..	..	10 55	12 20		..	..
Stapleton Road	..	8 15	9 15	..	..	..	11 0	12 25		..	..
Montpellier	6 40	8 20	9 20	9 35	..	..	11 5	12 30		..	..
Clifton Down arr.	6 45	8 25	9 25	9 40	..	..	11 10	12 36		..	..

UP.	T 1 2 P p.m.	1 2 p.m.	1 2 P p.m.	T 1 2 P p.m.	1 2 3 p.m	1 2 p.m.	1 2 P p.m	T 1 2 3 p.m.	1 2 P p.m.	1 2 3 p.m.	
Weston-s-Mare dep	12 40	1 45	3 6	3 30	4 50	5 20	..	7 20	8 0	9 10	..
Weston Junction	12 47	1 58	3 14	3 55	4 56	5 22	..	7 26	8 12	9 19	..
Worle	12 56	1 2 3 from Bristol	3 25	4 5	..	..	..	7 32	8 21	..	..
Yatton	1 5		3 35	4 15	5 11	5 47	6 45	7 40	8 31	9 31	..
Clevedon dep.	..		3 10	..	4 55	5 27	6 25	..	8 15	9 5	..
Clevedon arr.	2 26		4 15	..	5 25	6 20	6 55	..	8 45	9 45	..
Nailsea	1 15		3 45	4 25	5 20	..	6 54	..	8 41	..	..
Bourton	1 23		3 55	4 33	5 28	..	7 1	..	8 50	..	..
Bedminster	1 37	2 32	4 11	4 47	5 42	6 11	7 16	8 2	9 5	9 52	..
Bristol arr.	1 40	2 35	4 15	4 50	5 45	6 15	7 20	8 5	9 10	9 55	..
Bristol dep.	1 50	3 0	4 10	5 5	6 5	1 2 3 Cla.	7 30	8 15	—	—	..
Lawrence Hill	1 55	3 5	4 15	5 10	6 10		7 35	8 20	..	..	..
Stapleton Road	2 0	3 10	4 20	5 15	6 15		7 40	8 25	..	..	..
Montpellier	2 5	3 15	4 25	5 20	6 20		7 45	8 30	..	..	..
Clifton Down arr.	2 10	3 20	4 30	5 25	6 25		7 50	8 35	..	..	..

SUNDAYS. (UP) and FARES From Weston-s-Mare.

UP.	1 2 P p.m.	1 2 3 p.m.	1 2 3 p.m.	1 2 3 p.m.	1 2 p.m.	1	2	3	Par	1 Ret.	2 Ret.
Weston-s-Mare dep	12 29	..	..	..	5 25						
Weston Junction	12 38	..	..	..	5 37	0/4	0/3	0/1½	..	0/6	0/4
Worle	12 48	..	..	..	..	1/0	0/9	0/4½	..	1/6	1/2
Yatton	12 56	..	..	..	5 49	1/8	1/4	0/8	..	2/4	1/9
Clevedon dep.	12 44	..	..	..	5 35	2/6	2/0	1/0	..	3/6	2/7
Clevedon arr.	1 8	..	..	..	6 1						
Nailsea	1 5	..	..	..	5 59	2/6	2/0	1/0	..	3/6	2/7
Bourton	..	..	..	..	..	3/0	2/6	1/2½	..	4/0	3/0
Bedminster	1 27	..	..	..	6 17	3/9	3 0	1/6	..	5/0	3/8
Bristol arr.	1 33	..	..	..	6 20	..	..	..	..	..	..
Bristol dep.	2 0	3 30	5 0	6 0	7 45	..	..	..	..	..	..
Lawrence Hill	2 5	3 35	5 5	6 5	7 50	..	..	..	..	..	..
Stapleton Road	2 10	3 40	5 10	6 10	7 55	..	..	..	..	..	..
Montpellier	2 15	3 45	5 15	6 15	8 0	4/3	3/4	1/10½	..	5/9	4/2
Clifton Down arr.	2 20	3 50	5 20	6 20	8 5	4/3	3/4	1/11	..	5/9	4/

S Slip Carriage detached at Yatton at 5 35 p.m. M Market Passengers conveyed to Bristol by these Trains on Thursdays. T These Trains run thro' without change of carriage at Bristol Joint Station or at Weston-super-Mare Junction. On Wednesdays a Train leaves Bristol for Yatton, Clevedon, Worle, Weston Junction and Weston-super-Mare at 11.30 p.m.

The Portishead branch had an initial service of six trains each way soon increased to eight. On 8 July 1929 a half-hourly service was introduced, one train starting from Temple Meads and the other from Ashton Gate, trains crossing at Pill or Portbury Shipyard. Because of this more intensive service, only having one platform at Portishead led to operating problems, so the carriage loop was converted into a passenger loop to serve a second platform which came into use on 9 March 1930. The branch closed to passengers on 7 September 1964. Until 1915 a steam railmotor ran seven trips on the Henbury line each way daily except Sundays, but Temple Meads was so crowded that only two Down and three Up Henbury trains could use it, the others terminating at Stapleton Road. The Henbury line was also used by through trains between London and Avonmouth connecting with Canadian and Jamaican steamers. The line was closed to regular passenger traffic on 23 November 1964.

Initially the Bristol Port Railway & Pier ran six trains each way daily and five Up and four Down on Sundays. Weekly passenger services from Bristol to Clifton Down began on 1 October 1874 with 13 run by the MR from Mangotsfield and 10 by the GWR from Temple Meads. On Sundays no MR service

Above:
The 1877 timetable for trains between Clifton Down and Weston-super-Mare.

Left:
Class 1P 0-4-4T No 1389 at Kingswood Junction with a Mangotsfield–Clifton Down train, on 6 March 1936.
S. Miles Davey, courtesy P. G. Davey

Opposite:
First class saloon No 303 bearing the roof board: 'Imperial Direct West India Mail Service Jamaica Via Avonmouth'. *Author's collection*

operated, but the GWR ran seven trains. In February 1876 a through service was started between Clifton Down and Weston-super-Mare. When Clifton Down trains began running through to Avonmouth the GWR continued to run from Temple Meads, but the Midland started from St Philip's and ran via Clifton Junction and Easton Road Junction to the BSWUR, these two junctions being laid specially for the service. After nearly a month it ceased, but the service from Mangotsfield and Fishponds continued until March 1941, with a break from January 1917 to May 1919. In August 1887 six trains ran each way between Temple Meads and Avonmouth, plus 26 Down and 24 Up to Clifton Down, and 11 Down and 12 Up from Fishponds to Clifton Down. Prior to World War 1 a through train ran from Bath (Queen Square) to Clifton Down composed of Somerset & Dorset Railway coaches hauled by a Midland engine. With the closure of the Hotwells line in 1922, six Down and four Up additional trains were provided between Clifton Down and Avonmouth Dock. From 23 June 1928 many of the Avonmouth trains were extended to Severn Beach, a developing riverside resort. By 1947 the service to Avonmouth had increased to 33 each way and 18 on Sundays. Regular interval services began on 3 January 1955 with two single ex-GWR diesel railcars running singly, a GWR three-car unit and other trains steam-worked. Trains left Temple Meads every hour, with some extras at peak periods. On weekdays through workmen's services were run to Portishead and to Keynsham & Somerdale. As a result of the June 1961 fare increase which lost the railway a considerable volume of traffic, a reduced timetable was inaugurated from 5 March 1962. This poorer service lost yet more traffic and the schoolchildren's train was withdrawn. This was unfortunate as the railway's chief asset, Clifton Down Tunnel, enabled trains to beat the bus journey between the city centre and northwest Bristol by 15–20min. About 1911 through fast excursion trains were run from Clifton Down to London, these often departing at 4am and arriving back 24hr later. A special football service was run from Clifton Down to Ashton Gate near Bristol City football ground, while on Bank Holidays normal services were suspended and through trains were run to Weston-super-Mare. On these days all engines carried a disc on the buffer beam, a cross denoting a special, while ordinary trains bore an oval. In 1938 the LMS attempted to popularise Severn Beach and ran through excursions via Clifton Down from Redditch, Great Malvern, Birmingham and Gloucester. Excursions to Clifton Down for Bristol Zoo, known as 'monkey specials' were always popular, a total of

340,000 passengers being dealt with at this station from 1958 until 1966, though the closure of the Welsh Valleys lines, coupled with the opening of the Severn Bridge in 1966 caused the traffic to decline by 54%. From 1971 'monkey specials' used the new chord line between Patchway Junction and Filton West Junction, obviating the need for a locomotive to run round the train at Stoke Gifford or Stapleton Road. This chord line was constructed from material recovered from Ashley Hill Junction to Narroways Hill Junction when that line was singled. 'Monkey specials' can no longer be run as the Henbury line is now freight only. Today the Severn Beach line is financially supported by the local county council and provides the only public transport between Severn Beach and Avonmouth. Posters help develop traffic, announcing 'Explore the Severn Beach Line' and extolling features of interest: Severn Beach; the second Severn crossing; Clifton Down — the Downs and zoo; Montpelier — shopping facilities; Sea Mills — remains of Roman harbour and riverside walk; and Temple Meads — The Exploratory. In the autumn of 1995, owing to increased costs brought about by high rolling stock and track access charges, on Mondays to Fridays trains from Temple Meads between 06.00 and 09.00 and 16.00–19.00 terminate at Avonmouth so that just one Sprinter can work an hourly service. It is only just possible to operate this as the 3–9min turnround time at Temple Meads and three minutes at Avonmouth do not allow for delays. With one-unit operation, the arrival time at Temple Meads is inconvenient for some passengers unless working flexitime, as there is no arrival between 08.05 and 09.05. At periods when trains do not run through to Severn Beach, Valley Travel Ltd (its depot is on the site of the former Lawrence Hill goods yard) provides a minibus link. On Saturdays an extra Sprinter is available and so two are used, crossing at Clifton Down.

The first sorting coaches, four in number, were ordered by the GPO in July 1841 for use between London and Bristol followed by the inauguration of the world's first special postal train on 1 February 1855. Leaving Paddington at 8.46pm it arrived at Temple Meads at 12.30am, its Up counterpart leaving Bristol at 12.35am and arriving at 4.10. It was usually a very light train of two sorting coaches and a van; the vans were worked beyond Bristol to and from Plymouth by ordinary passenger trains. From June 1869 it ceased to be solely for postal traffic and one first class coach was attached; accommodation was so limited that even directors who wished to travel by this train had to apply for a special pass. A Plymouth–Bristol TPO commenced on 1 December 1859 and connected with the North Mail, on 11 February 1896 becoming the Bristol & Penzance TPO (North Mail), the Bristol & Plymouth TPO on 14 April 1930 and ceased running on 3 March 1972. In the days of Ocean Mails from Plymouth a van was slipped at Bedminster for Bristol. In March 1855 the Bristol–Newcastle mail was inaugurated, the van being the only item of coaching stock to carry the letters M&NEJS (Midlands & North Eastern Joint Stock). By 1885 it used the TPO apparatus at Fishponds. The TPOs were suspended during World War 2. Today Temple Meads receives 12 Res (Rail express systems) trains daily from Cardiff, Glasgow, Newcastle, Old Oak Common, Penzance, Swansea and Wolverhampton.

The Bristol to Edinburgh Motorail service was withdrawn from 28 May 1995. This was the remnant of a Newton Abbot to Stirling service which carried a portion from Bristol. An ancestor of the Raildrive car service in the 1840s saw post horses kept ready at Temple Meads to draw carriages from the Clifton district to Temple Meads.

On summer Saturdays some Up holiday trains used the Avoiding line to ease congestion at Temple Meads. It was a mixed blessing as a train had to foul the Down line to reach it; then wait its turn to get over the Bath–Bristol line at North Somerset Junction and blocked the Up line in order to attain the South Wales line at Dr Day's Bridge Junction where it fouled the Down South Wales line. Trains using this route tended to lose time and the only solution to the difficulty would have been to have built flyovers. This would have proved difficult and uneconomic as they were only required for a maximum of 15 days a year. One interesting train which used the Avoiding line in 1952 was the 9.52am (SO) from Weston-super-Mare to Birmingham New Street, usually worked throughout by a Midland engine which did not regain its own metals until Yate.

Although passenger sailings from Bristol itself did not develop on a large scale, there were some in the first half of this century from Avonmouth. Quite early in Avonmouth's history a passenger platform and waiting room were provided at the landward end of the East Pier and later a timber passenger station was built at the South Pier, the GWR manning the booking office. Boat trains in connection with the West Indies service ran fortnightly, Port of Bristol Authority's locomotives working GWR coaches over the dock lines. In 1911, 25,165 passengers travelled to Avonmouth by rail and only 8,185 in the reverse direction, the difference approximately indicating the number of emigrants. Trains carrying emigrants to the docks were required to be locked after passengers had alighted and not used again until after being disinfected. Latterly the West Indies traffic did not warrant a whole train and just two or three coaches were attached to a Paddington–Bristol express and were worked specially to Avonmouth. The passenger station there was destroyed in an air raid during World War 2 and a platform at the South Tranship Shed was used subsequently. The last boat train was worked on 26 August 1964. Sometimes Campbell's White Funnel Line ran paddle boat excursions from the docks, passengers arriving by special train.

NUMBER OF TRAINS DAILY FROM BRISTOL

To	Sept 1850	July 1913	July 1939	May 1980	Oct 1995
London	9	15	12 + 1SX	26	26 (22 Sats)
Plymouth	No through	9	12 + 1MX + 7SO	15 + 5 SO + 1 MO	16
Portsmouth	trains on these	4 from TM	1 from TM 3 from S Rd + 2SO S Rd	7 + 2SO	16
Cardiff	lines	10 from TM 3 from S Rd	17 + 1 SX TM 7 + 1 FX S Rd	17 + 4 SO	35 (Sats 23)
Birmingham	5	16	17 + 8 SO 1 from S Rd	15 + 1MX 7 SO 1FO	19 (Sats 15)

Right:
Diesel railcar No 8 near Horfield on a Temple Meads–Cardiff working, 29 September 1936. *S. Miles Davey, courtesy P. G. Davey*

Below right:
The 'X' dividing Platform No 11 (beyond the cross) from Platform No 12 (this side of the cross), 23 August 1995. *Author*

Below:
Signal indicating to platform staff that the starting signal is either yellow or green and so the 'Right Away' may be safely given, 31 October 1995. *Author*

In 1935 Temple Meads, the principal Bristol station, was used by over 400 passenger trains daily, it being the most important exchange station on the GWR with routes converging from London, Exeter, Southampton, Bournemouth, Weymouth, South Wales and the Midlands. Over 5 million passengers used it that year, a further three and a half million using the suburban stations of Stapleton Road, Lawrence Hill and Bedminster, while 10 million passengers passed through on their journeys. In December 1995 the number of daily train movements at Temple Meads were:

Rail Express Systems	27
Regional Railways	195
Great Western Trains	68
Cross Country Trains	32

Following the closure of the Brunel train shed in September 1965 the platforms were renumbered starting from the north and working south, instead of the reverse order as had been the case with the 1935 renumbering. Today No 1 is the east end bay, just long enough for four Sprinter cars. Normally used by Severn Beach trains, it is sometimes used by a late-running Portsmouth–Cardiff train. This is because passengers connecting with a north train can just cross the platform instead of using the subway and thus save about five minutes on a connection. No 2 is the parcels bay at the west end of the station used for mail and Red Star, the office for the latter being in the adjacent Collett House. The other 10 platforms are long and of the through variety and subdivided into two. The actual division is marked by a suspended rectangular illuminated sign bearing a

Above:
47500 *Great Western* heads the 16.25 Temple Meads–Taunton, normally a Sprinter working, 16 June 1988. *Author*

Left:
'Hymek' D7023 at Portishead with the 5.15pm to Temple Meads, 28 August 1964.
E. T. Gill/Revd Brian Arman collection

Right:
Old and new signalboxes at Ashley Hill Junction on 3 April 1959. The new box opened on 10 May 1959 and closed on 27 February 1966. The DMU is working between Temple Meads and Severn Beach. *E. T. Gill/Revd Brian Arman collection*

Below right:
A coupling problem at Temple Meads: No 158835, right, detached from the four-car 09.00 Brighton–Tenby, strengthening No 158819, left, the 11.55 Cardiff–Penzance, 23 August 1995. *Author*

black 'X' on a white ground and treated by train crews as a danger signal. Odd-numbered platforms are situated at the east end of the station and even numbers at the west. HST and DMU drivers receive a buzzer signal in the cab when they are to start, but because the curved platforms hamper visibility, there is a special departure procedure for locomotive-hauled trains. Not more than two minutes before the booked departure time, the platform chargeperson presses a 'Train Ready to Start' button which notifies the panel box. An 'RA' (Right Away) sign, operated by a button pressed by platform staff after giving RA to the guard first, lights up beside the starting signal and the driver opens up. As a safety precaution platform staff must not give 'Right Away' to the guard unless the starting signal is off and as this cannot be seen due to the curve, a white light for the staff in the centre of the platform reads 'OFF' when the signal is yellow or green. All platform staff are in radio contact which saves the time and trouble of finding a phone and is particularly valuable at busy periods.

Temple Meads has a considerable and growing commuter traffic, especially to and from Keynsham, Bath and Chippenham; to and from Parkway and Yate and all stations towards Weston-super-Mare; also Severn Tunnel Junction, Newport and Cardiff.

Quite a variety of trains can be seen: HSTs, Sprinters, Super Sprinters and Pacers plus locomotive-hauled freight and parcels trains and the ubiquitous Class 08 shunter.

In the early 1900s a wide variety of coaches belonging to various companies could be seen at Temple Meads. Apart from GWR and MR stock there were through Somerset & Dorset coaches to Bournemouth; Great Central coaches on through

trains from Ilfracombe to Halifax and Leeds, from York/Sheffield via Banbury, and Taunton to Leicester; London & North Western coaches from Plymouth to Manchester; a West Coast Joint Stock coach ran from Exeter to Glasgow; while Caledonian coaches ran from Bristol to Edinburgh. With the reduction in the number of locomotive-hauled trains, carriage sidings at Ashton Meadows, Dr Day's, Filton West Junction, Malago Vale, Marsh Pond and St Philip's, have all been rendered redundant. Until 1988 Malago Vale sidings could clean and store up to 133 coaches and also carry out minor repairs such as replacing broken steps and worn brake blocks. A shore plug was provided for electric heating, while steam came either from a boiler house or a portable boiler. Kingsland Road and Pylle Hill sidings are now used for stabling coaches on the occasions when this becomes necessary.

As Bristol is an important junction, signalling is vital. In 1909 Temple Meads was controlled by four boxes, two of which contained 105 levers each. With the extension of the station in 1935 the signalling was renewed. Bristol Temple Meads East powerbox was the largest on the GWR and replaced two mechanical boxes: Temple Meads East and South Wales Junction. It had 23 block bells, each having a different tone and was in communication with no less than seven adjacent boxes. Its architecture was 'avant-garde' and still looked modern when replaced 35 years later. It had three storeys, whereas the similar West and Loco boxes had but two. The exteriors were of red brick in Flemish bond relieved by white stone lintels and sills. Points were operated by Metro Vickers GRS model 5A dc machines fed from a 120V battery situated in the cabin. The East box had 368 'levers' which were actually slides pulled to halfway position where they locked until the point or colour light signal had functioned correctly, when they could then be pulled out to their fullest extent. Three special class signalmen were always on duty plus a booking boy. Bristol West had 328 levers and 20 bells and was also manned by three men and a boy.

With a view to economies through closing 70 signalboxes and saving 343 staff, Multiple Aspect Signalling, operated from one box at Bristol, was installed in 1970 at a cost of about £4 million and controlled 114 route miles from Cogload Junction to Bradford Junction, Corsham, Badminton, Charfield, Pilning and Avonmouth. The resignalling would have been hard to justify financially without track rationalisation, especially that at Temple Meads which has allowed trains to be handled more expeditiously at fewer platforms, the simplified layout also permitting the speed limit approaching the station to be raised from 10 to 25mph. Through programming of locomotives largely obviated engine changes at Temple Meads reducing the number of movements required, the average time a train spent at a platform being reduced from 18min in 1938 to 4min in 1976. In 1996 HSTs usually have about 3min while South Wales–Portsmouth trains, on which the driver changes cabs, have about 6min.

Below:
Temple Meads: loading rabbits into the luggage van of an evening express to Paddington on 5 November 1950. *Pursey Short*

Opposite above:
No 15303 working the 13.08 Temple Meads–Severn Beach stands at Platform No 1. On the far left is the 09.22 Penzance–Edinburgh. Above No 15303 is the MAS box, 31 October 1995. *Author*

Opposite below:
The main panel in the Bristol MAS box, 29 July 1980. *Author*

STATISTICS OF THE BRISTOL PANEL BOX WHEN OPENED

Number of point machines	243	
Number of controlled signals	(2, 3, & 4-aspect)	163
Number of automatic signals	(2, 3 & 4-aspect)	117
Number of track circuits (functional)	556	
Number of ground frames	50	
Number of level crossings	3	
Number of WR AWS ramps	200	
Number of BR AWS indicators	24	
Number of telephones — on signal posts	268	
— on ground frames etc	124	

The box has two separate consoles: the main covers Cogload Junction–Temple Meads–Corsham, also Bradford Junction and the former four-track section to Stapleton Road; while the subsidiary console deals with Stapleton Road–Pilning, Badminton and Charfield. Three-aspect multi-lens signals are used, but four-aspect signalling has been installed on certain sections where an improved headway is required — for example between Westerleigh and Stoke Gifford where the two tracks carry the former Midland service in addition to South Wales main line traffic, and also through the Temple Meads station area where closer spacing is required for crossing movements. Interlockings within three or four miles of Bristol are operated by individual circuits over a telephone type non-vital cable; beyond this distance, electronic time division multiplex equipment is used. Current supplies are obtained from the mains at various sites and transformed to 650V single-phase ac for distribution along the track. Lineside hot box detectors are installed on both lines at Coalpit Heath and at Nailsea on the Up. They alert signalmen at Bristol of up to four hot boxes on one train, together with their positions in the train. Normal staff on a shift is three signalmen at the main panel between 06.00 and 22.00 and one between 22.00 and 06.00; one at the subsidiary panel; and a panel supervisor.

In the event of the need to substitute for a passenger train, road coaches of R. C. Turner & Co whose depot adjoins the Res Barton Hill depot, are generally used since vehicles can be supplied within 20min.

The former Avon County Council promoted the Westway, a rapid transport network. The first stage is Line 1, a 32.5km-long line planned to link Bradley Stoke, (north of Bristol Parkway), Filton, Horfield and Ashley Down to Temple Meads and the city centre,

while south Bristol will be served by a loop from the city centre to Temple Meads, Barton Hill, Brislington, Hengrove, Hartcliffe and Bedminster back to the city centre. For about 80% of the route it will be segregated from other traffic. Future lines will serve Portishead, Severn Beach, Yate and possibly Bath.

It is anticipated that Westway Line 1 will save two million car journeys each year. It has yet to be finalised as to whether the system will use a conventional light rail system with 750V dc electric traction, or an electrically-powered guided light transit system as advocated by FirstBus Transit Developments Ltd. The abolition of Avon County Council on 31 March 1996 has meant that four new unitary authorities will be involved in Westway's future, but it is anticipated that in 1997 an Order will be granted for Line 1; construction will begin in 1999 and Line 1 will open in 2002. It is anticipated that up to 20% of funding for Westway will come from the private sector and that Westway will make a profit and not require a subsidy.

Although the privately-funded Advanced Transport for Avon Ltd obtained an Act in May 1989 for a line mainly following the existing disused track from Portishead to Wapping Wharf, Bristol, its efforts to raise money were unsuccessful and powers for construction lapsed. This route has now been given a lower priority.

Above:
No 43187 enters Temple Meads with the 10.45 Waterloo–Cardiff via Kensington, 31 October 1995. *Author*

Left:
Driver David Chambers, Derby, cleans the windscreen of No 43156 working the 08.26 Paignton–Newcastle, 31 October 1995. *Author*

DEVELOPMENT OF FREIGHT SERVICES

Bristol was the focal point of three broad gauge companies, the GWR, B&E and Bristol & Gloucester, but development of freight traffic was hampered by the fact that until the 1860s and 1870s there was no rail access to the docks. Lines to Avonmouth and Portishead were opened in 1865 and 1867 respectively, but at first handled passengers rather than freight.

Towards the end of the 19th century, as many ships were too large to navigate the river to Bristol, Avonmouth grew in importance. In 1890 it was selected as the port for the fortnightly Imperial West Indies mail service while in March 1901 the first consignment of bananas arrived, Elders & Fyffes inaugurating a fortnightly service for Port Limon, Costa Rica. Until 1967, when the traffic ceased, bananas were important. For instance in 1927, 75 banana ships arrived requiring 425 special trains at an average of $47\frac{1}{2}$ wagons each. In the winter months 600 GWR banana vans had to be preheated to 68°F and 10 fitted brake vans lettered 'Avonmouth RU' were allocated to this traffic. The LMS also ran banana trains, one leaving Avonmouth at 3.50pm and arriving St Pancras at 3.8am. Traffic in the years following World War 2 was heavy and when two banana boats arrived within a week, 700 vans required to be stored in the week prior to their arrival; tared (weighed empty); loaded and then grossed (weighed full). Wagons of loose straw, known as 'wagons of wind', came mainly from stations on the Badminton line.

Petroleum was another important commodity and

Above:
No 6836 *Estevarney Grange* (83D Laira) passes Temple Meads Loco Yard signalbox with a Down vacuum-fitted freight.
P. Q. Treloar collection

Left:
Banana van lettered 'Return to Avonmouth' preserved at the Didcot Railway Centre. *Author*

as early as 1911, 27 oil tanks were set in the vicinity of the docks and in 1919 an oil basin was added to the Royal Edward Docks. In 1964 $1^1/_2$ million tons of traffic were hauled over the Port of Bristol Authority's lines in 96,506 wagons by 21 PBA diesel and seven steam engines; this, however, decreased to none in 1983 when the system closed. For instance, cattle food which used to go by rail to small country stations, most of which were closed in the Beeching era, now goes by road.

Avonmouth was very important during both world wars. In addition to its normal trains, extra traffic had to be catered for: for example, horses and mules destined for the army, 89 truck loads being dispatched on one day alone, and 65,956 mules arriving in less than eight months. An example of the troop traffic can be seen in the figures for 7–11 February 1915 when 92 trains consisting of 2,093 loaded coaches, vans, horse boxes, cattle vans and open trucks were hauled by PBA engines from the Exchange

KINGSWOOD JUNCTION AND AVONMOUTH.

WEEKDAYS.

Miles	Classification ..	G		J		G		J	J	J	J	H	G		G	H	G	
		11.50 p.m. E & B. from Bristol.	To work 1.35 a.m. to Barnwood.	6.30 a.m. from Westerleigh.	Ashley Hill Junc. arr. 7*15	8.15 a.m. E & B. from Bristol.	To work 9.30 a.m. to Barnwood.	9.30 a.m. from Westerleigh.	11.5 a.m. from Westerleigh.	5.30 p.m. from Westerleigh.	5.30 p.m. from Westerleigh.	6.57 p.m. from Bath.	7.20 p.m. Engine & Brake from Bristol.	To work 8.00 p.m. to Water Orton.	8.30 p.m. Engine & Brake from Fish Ponds.	8.20 p.m. from Bath.	10.10 p.m. E & B. from Bristol.	To work 11.40 p.m. to Water Orton.
	Target No. ..			34				44	31	31	39	42			39	42		
		MX				Q				SO	SX	SO	SX		SX	SX	SX	
		a.m.		a.m.		a.m.		a.m.	a.m.	p.m.	p.m.	p.m.	p.m.		p.m.	p.m.	p.m.	
0	KINGSWOOD JC.	12* 1		7 0		8*18		9 43	11 30	5 47	6 0	7 15	7*35		8 53	9 7	10*22	
1	S'ton Rd. Gas Wks.	..		..		..		9 50	..	..	..	..	..		..	..	..	
1¾	Ashley Hill Jc.	12 10		7*25		8 23		..	11 47	5 59	6 9	7 33	7 43		8 59	9 20	10 37	
2½	Montpelier .. arr.	..		7 29		..		..	..	..	..	..	..		..	..	..	
	dep.	..		8 5		..		..	..	..	..	..	..		..	..	..	
3½	Clifton Down......	12 14		8 10		8 36		..	11 54	6 7	6 17	7 38	7 50		9 3	9 30	10 41	
7	Shirehampton.....	..		..		..		..	..	..	..	..	..		..	..	..	
7½	A'mouth Dock Jc.	12 26		..		8 52		..	12 15	6 25	6 34	7 56	8 3		9 15	9 48	10 53	
8½	AVONMOUTH. arr.	12 30		..		8 55		..	12 20	6 30	6 36	8 0	8 7		9 17	9 52	10 57	

SUNDAYS.

WEEKDAYS.

Miles	Classification ..	G	J	J	J	J	H	J	H
		Engine and Brake to Westerleigh.	Empties to Westerleigh.	1.40 p.m. from Royal Ed. Yard to Westerleigh.	To Fish Ponds.	To Fish Ponds.	To Bath.	To Fish Ponds.	To Bath.
	Target No. ..	44	34	31	39	31	42	39	42
					SX	SO	SO	SX	SX
		a.m.	a.m.	p.m.	p.m.	p.m.	p.m.	p.m.	p.m.
0	AVONMOUTH ......dep.	..	..	2 40	7 30	7 30	10 25	10 25	11 10
¾	Avonmouth Dock Junc.	..	..	2 43	7 34	7 34	10 28	10 28	11 16
1¼	Shirehampton..........	..	..	..	..	..	..	..	..
5½	Clifton Down...........	..	10 40	3 8	7 37	7 37	10 30	10 38	11 34
6¼	Montpelier........ arr.	..	10 47	..	..	..	..	..	..
	dep.	..	10 57	..	..	..	..	..	..
6¾	Ashley Hill Junc.	..	11 0	3 15	8 4	8 4	10 37	11 4	11 42
7¼	Stapleton Rd. Gas Wks.	10 20	..	..	..	..	..	..	..
8¼	KINGSWOOD JUNC. arr.	10 30	11 15	3 25	8 18	8 18	11 10	11 20	12* 0

SUNDAYS.

G 17

Top:
0-6-2T No 5665 pictured at Avonmouth on 21 December 1964.
E. T. Gill/Revd Brian Arman collection

Above:
Freight train timetable Kingswood Junction–Avonmouth, commencing 21 September 1953.

Right:
Imperial Smelting Co Ltd's No 3 at Avonmouth on 24 August 1956. The legend at the foot of the bunker reads: 'The Imperial Smelting Co Ltd Avonmouth'. No 3 was built by Hudswell, Clarke in 1948 and scrapped in December 1960. *Revd Alan Newman*

Above:
New Hudswell, Clarke-built, Port of Bristol Authority No D2005 *Celidon* while being delivered new on a Pickford's low-loader on the A38 at Twyning, north of Tewkesbury, 9 August 1956.
Revd Alan Newman

Left:
Ashton, a PBA locomotive at Avonmouth *c*1958. *Ashton*, built by Peckett in 1934, was scrapped in March 1966.
R. J. Cannon/Author's collection

Sidings to the embarkation berth. During World War 2 Avonmouth again became of vital importance to the country as it was one of the ports to receive supplies from the USA. The PBA's fleet of 2,150 open wagons and vans at Avonmouth and 80 at Portishead declined by 1980 to 80 at Avonmouth alone and none today. Some wagons were for internal use only, while others bearing a red spot were allowed to travel over BR lines.

Until March 1995 fertilizer arrived from Immingham to the Norsk Hydro distribution warehouses adjacent to Britannia Zinc Ltd's works, the latter company providing the twice weekly shunting service. The Britannia Zinc plant started during World War 1 and until about 1972 also operated a narrow gauge system. Several standard gauge tank engines were operated until 1959/60 when two Sentinel four-wheel diesel-hydraulic engines, Nos 6 and 7, were purchased and worked until traffic ceased on 31 December 1995. Until 1966 imported zinc and lead concentrates were brought by rail from Avonmouth, but that year a conveyor was opened between the docks and the works. Until recently drums of hydrofluoric acid were conveyed by rail, sulphuric acid in tank wagons and lead dross in sheeted open wagons. Industry coke was brought daily from Margam until early 1995 and until December 1995 about 400 tonnes of lead in 2-tonne blocks was sent to the Continent by rail weekly in VTG wagons hired from Tiphook. Some curves were very sharp and required flange oilers, while to avoid buffer interlocking, a coupling bar was used to keep buffers well apart. It is expected that the system will reopen.

An automated bulk coal terminal has recently been opened at Avonmouth. Coal from various countries is unloaded at Portbury by two cranes and sent on conveyor under the river to Avonmouth where it is transferred to a hopper about 200ft in height, at St Andrew's Road. Sensors identify the type of wagon approaching the hopper and an electrically-operated hydraulic system feeds the correct amount of coal into each wagon. A control cabin at the base of the hopper and set above the tracks has television screens so that the automatic loading can be checked. The operation is remarkably clean and dust-free. Some coal can be loaded at 1mph while other types require a speed of 1/2mph. Following clearance tests on 25 June 1993, No 60079 hauled the first coal train from Avonmouth to Didcot

Left:
Van at Britannia Zinc Ltd's works, Avonmouth, with 2-tonne ingots destined for the Continent, 9 November 1995. *Author*

Below left:
Britannia Zinc Ltd's No 6 in the workshop, 9 November 1995. *Author*

Above:
Albright & Wilson Ltd's Peckett Works No 1611 of 1923 at Portishead on 22 May 1964. *Revd Alan Newman*

Right:
In semi-rural surroundings new Fiat cars await unloading at the Chittening Estate Siding, 7 March 1996. Notice the wheel chocks removed and placed against the wagon sides. Coloured lines painted on the deck assist steering the cars away from the sides. *Author*

on 21 July 1993. Normally four Didcot and two Aberthaw MGR trains run five days a week and only load on Saturdays if trains have been lost during the week through locomotive or plant failure. A Class 58 or Class 60 usually works to Didcot and a Class 56 or Class 60 to Aberthaw, train lengths being 45 and 36 wagons respectively. The engine release road is owned by Railtrack, but the eight yard sidings belong to Bristol Port Co and National Power. This yard is unusual in that it is motorised — only two points are moved by hand, all the rest being operated by phoning to St Andrew's panel signalbox.

Trains of liquid petroleum gas (LPG) from Furzebrook, on the Isle of Purbeck, to Hallen Marsh started on 27 November 1990. Initially Class 47-worked, they are now generally headed by a Class 58 or Class 60. Currently two trains run daily. Three sets of wagons are involved; the empties being removed and the full wagons left for their contents to be discharged into spheres. Some LPG is distributed throughout the southwest by road while the remainder is exported by sea.

153382

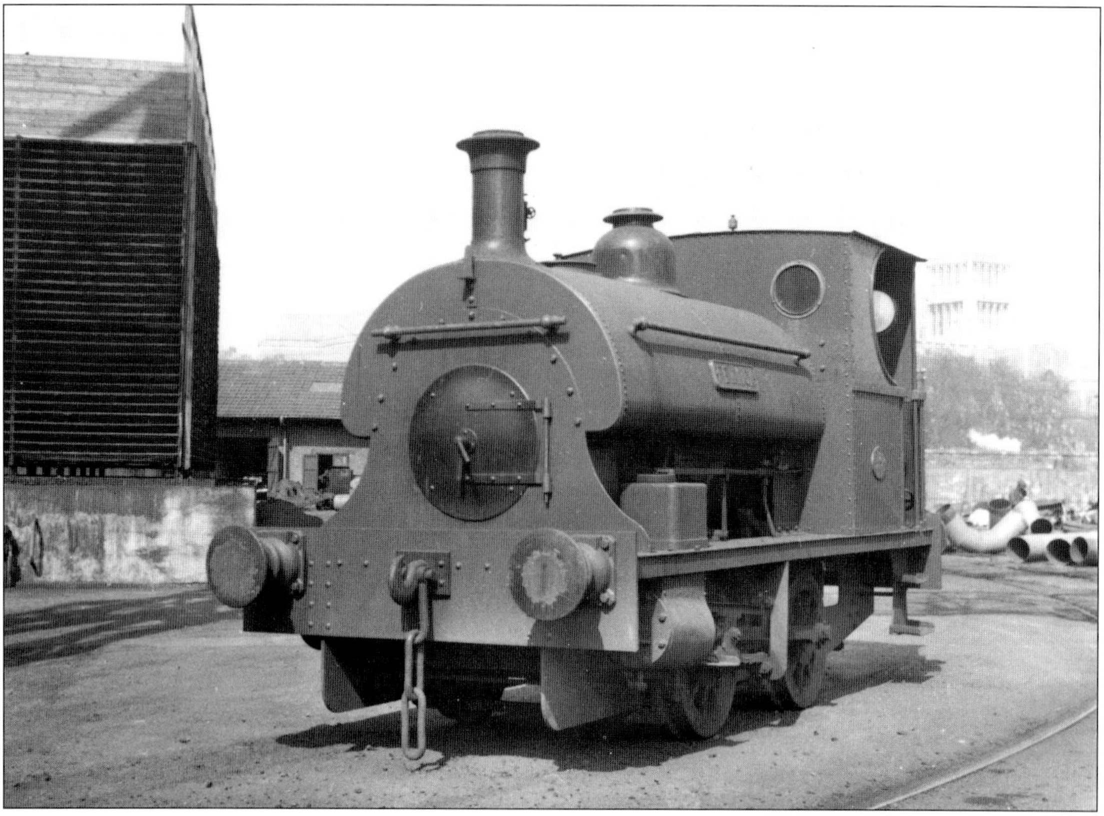

Left:
No 153382 approaches St Andrew's Road with the 13.00 Severn Beach-Temple Meads, 9 October 1995. On the right, the coal sidings can be seen. *Author*

Below left:
Fenwick, Peckett Works No 1221 of 1911, at Canon's Marsh gasworks, 21 April 1955. She was scrapped in 1960. *Revd Alan Newman*

Right:
On 7 March 1996 wagons for Aberthaw power station emerge from below the hopper at St Andrew's Road after being loaded. The control room can be seen above. *Author*

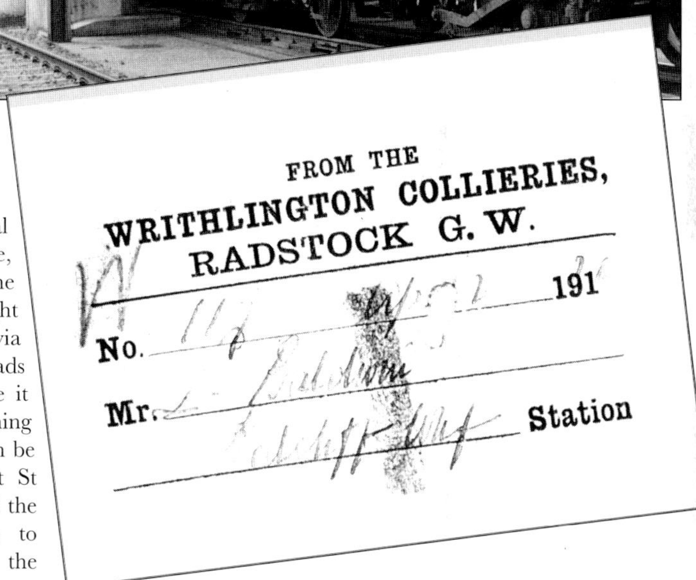

FROM THE
WRITHLINGTON COLLIERIES,
RADSTOCK G. W.

191

No.

Mr.

Station

Below right:
Wagon label Writhlington Colliery, Radstock, to Redcliff Wharf, Bristol, 11 April 1922.

On 9 March 1995 the first cars of an initial 12,000 car contract arrived at Chittening Estate, Hallen Marsh, from Turin travelling via the Channel Tunnel to the Wembley European Freight Operating Centre. From there it travels via Reading, Swindon and Filton to Temple Meads where the engine is run round the train to take it back to Filton with the cars arriving at Chittening with their bonnets facing the rear so that they can be driven off forwards. When the train arrives at St Andrew's Road, the locomotive is run round and the wagon couplings unscrewed to enable them to negotiate the tight curves when pushed into the unloading sidings. The cars on the top deck are driven down a hydraulic ramp placed at the rear of the train and then the lower deck is emptied. The cars are then taken to Portbury to be distributed by road. The empty STVA wagons are sent to Washwood Heath, Longbridge or Cowley and return to Italy through the Channel Tunnel loaded with Rover cars. The service to Chittening is on a Thursday, usually weekly. In 1995 Railfreight ran 61 trains from Turin to Avonmouth, each carrying an average of 192 cars.

ICI Severnside has two Yorkshire Engine 0-6-0 diesel-electrics, *Kildare* and *Iburndale*. As the rail system is temporarily out of use, these locomotives were away on loan in February 1996. Grasmere Railfreight Terminal is likely to open near Hallen Marsh in the near future.

Goods traffic on the Portishead line was less important than that from Avonmouth; timber, grain, beans and petroleum being the main items. Phosphorus was manufactured at Portishead and the finished product distributed in specially-built rail tank wagons. A woodpulp terminal opened at Portishead dock in the early 1970s and until December 1976 pulp was loaded into a bulk train for the journey to Marsh Pond, Bristol. The last cement train ran to Portishead on 3 April 1981 and subsequently a few trains of cars imported at Portbury Docks were forwarded by rail.

The BNSR served the Radstock coalfield and in 1913 eight Down goods and mineral trains ran over the line compared with nine passenger trains. With

Continued on page 58

TRAFFIC DEALT WITH AT STATIONS.

BRISTOL DIVISION.
(Steventon to Highbridge.

Passenger Train Traffic

Station	Year	Staff: Supervisory and Wages (all Grades)	Staff: Paybill Expenses	Total Receipts	Tickets issued	Season Tickets	Receipts: Passengers (including Season Tickets, etc.)	Receipts: Parcels	Receipts: Miscellaneous	Receipts: Total
		No.	£	£	No.	No.	£	£	£	£
Steventon to	Highbridge	(contd.)								
Bristol (Lawrence Hill) Goods (§)	1903	*	*	24 414						
	1913	64	4,052	48,231						
	1923	78	12,712	85,127						
	1924	87	13,543	82,919						
	1925	87	13,937	83,123						
	1926	89	13,866	80,287						
	1927	89	14,192	83,164						
	1928	90	13,705	80,256						
	1929	89	13,545	82,156						
	1930	89	13,350	75,888						
	1931	87	13,070	74,001						
	1932	§	§	60,307						
	1933	¶	¶	59,914						
Bristol (Temple Meads) Passenger. (‡)	1903	434	27,234	242,706	1,047,925	*	175,873	38,370	28,462	242,706
	1913	318	28,085	260,174	1,110,898	*	201,595	38,457	20,122	260,174
	1923	359	60,638	484,511	1,215,840	7,425	373,329	84,676	26,506	484,511
	1924	348	59,891	497,591	1,211,070	7,536	390,244	79,872	27,475	497,591
	1925	310	56,134	479,784	1,211,676	8,413	370,484	80,798	28,502	479,784
	1926	300	52,506	446,908	1,087,574	8,763	333,405	83,363	30,140	446,908
	1927	333	61,965	451,018	1,106,613	9,505	338,496	85,054	27,468	451,018
	1928	†330	†61,789	451,225	1,100,184	9,547	334,837	87,208	29,180	451,225
	1929	†337	†61,745	442,121	1,071,039	7,762	323,819	90,484	27,818	442,121
	1930	†332	†64,164	431,277	1,022,835	7,970	315,821	89,404	26,052	431,277
	1931	†338	†61,831	403,911	916,538	6,774	293,811	85,987	24,113	403,911
	1932	†340	†60,410	381,344	844,269	5,934	277,067	79,418	24,859	381,344
	1933	†336	†64,937	387,871	856,778	6,076	270,882	91,926	25,063	387,871
Bristol (Temple Meads) Goods.	1903	*	*	688,163						
	1913	969	70,877	736,257						
	1923	948	161,672	1,154,785						
	1924	990	165,050	1,102,867						
	1925	990	172,190	1,129,094						
	1926	996	168,798	1,101,749						
	1927	994	177,004	1,163,844						
	1928	994	182,016	1,153,540						
	1929	994	183,674	1,127,758						
	1930	1,035	186,100	1,060,706						
	1931	1,037	187,270	1,002,945						
	1932	1,097	187,368	890,493						
	1933	1,065	183,935	890,601						
Bedminster ..	1903	21	1,725	4,636	56,039	*	3,894	455	287	4,636
	1913	10	831	5,904	70,928	*	5,783	109	12	5,904
	1923	11	2,258	12,106	139,470	120	11,750	271	85	12,106
	1924	11	2,018	13,829	141,132	110	13,529	249	51	13,829
	1925	11	2,067	15,236	167,789	169	14,920	242	74	15,236
	1926	11	1,887	12,660	133,024	151	12,387	241	32	12,660
	1927	13	2,167	13,399	131,946	140	13,056	254	89	13,399
	1928	13	2,306	12,257	130,174	128	11,944	262	51	12,257
	1929	13	2,336	11,487	125,174	91	11,145	253	89	11,487
	1930	13	2,426	9,263	108,002	57	9,029	198	36	9,263
	1931	13	2,319	8,210	94,548	66	8,004	188	18	8,210
	1932	13	2,318	7,236	90,153	66	7,079	140	17	7,236
	1933	13	2,116	8,207	94,878	100	8,068	125	14	8,207
Parson Street Platform.				Opened	August,	1927.				
	1927	Included with Bedminster.		666	5,966	3	632	33	1	666
	1928			4,763	51 981	11	4,653	105	5	4,763
	1929			5,868	66,373	21	5,778	88	2	5,868
	1930			5,336	60,648	24	5,230	93	13	5,336
	1931			4,741	51,856	18	4,622	106	13	4,741
	1932			4,917	54,500	30	4,830	75	3	4,917
	1933			5,871	67,203	16	5,775	92	4	5,871

Goods Train Traffic

Station	Year	Forwarded: Coal and Coke "Charged."	Forwarded: Other Minerals	Forwarded: General Merchandise	Received: Coal and Coke "Charged."	Received: Other Minerals	Received: General Merchandise	Coal and Coke "Not Charged" (Forwarded and Received)	Total Goods Tonnage	Total Receipts (excluding "Not Charged" Coal and Coke)	Livestock (Forwarded and Received)	Total Carted Tonnage (included in Total Goods Tonnage)
		Tons.	Tons.	Tons.	Tons.	Tons.	Tons.	Tons.	Tons.	£	Wagons.	Tons.
Bristol (Lawrence Hill) Goods (§)	1903	43	1,207	15,257	30,551	4,270	13,281	14,294	79,083	24,414	—	11,619
	1913	105	3,242	28,775	26,130	4,035	21,968	32,347	117,602	48,231	—	29,036
	1923	95	3,836	25,835	12,982	4,666	30,493	33,716	110,823	85,127	—	32,508
	1924	210	1,968	29,001	20,169	2,824	31,744	35,378	121,294	82,919	—	35,592
	1925	147	2,065	29,073	14,366	3,675	31,404	42,419	123,209	83,123	—	36,482
	1926	204	2,611	27,069	9,024	3,199	29,990	28,441	100,838	80,287	—	35,493
	1927	140	3,969	28,058	8,629	3,900	29,360	38,006	112,158	83,164	—	35,247
	1928	208	3,237	27,055	8,245	2,752	30,054	33,927	105,478	80,256	—	34,427
	1929	97	3,654	27,237	8,019	3,456	31,072	36,320	110,763	82,156	—	36,842
	1930	60	2,653	26,295	6,738	3,008	30,904	41,016	111,086	75,888	—	33,866
	1931	5	2,788	26,662	7,560	2,807	30,348	45,884	110,049	74,001	—	33,911
	1932	23	3,222	23,395	5,166	1,470	22,245	42,188	97,709	60,307	—	27,336
	1933	22	3,362	22,608	4,294	1,425	21,282	41,966	94,949	59,914	—	27,077
Bristol (Temple Meads) Goods.	1903	45,649	207,689	875,275	111,716	241,304	221,585	72,811	1,776,030	688,163	14,170	371,873
	1913	34,994	70,956	893,903	81,741	36,815	375,765	90,194	1,584,458	736,257	10,811	446,358
	1923	10,854	41,837	654,136	74,367	57,570	411,318	144,031	1,403,622	1,154,785	7,200	398,217
	1924	4,402	45,473	667,360	92,716	73,762	407,809	164,074	1,456,658	1,102,867	7,701	417,218
	1925	6,013	38,966	683,502	82,257	77,017	427,347	184,403	1,499,615	1,129,094	5,508	420,914
	1926	26,514	43,473	654,599	58,159	78,232	415,191	159,834	1,436,302	1,101,749	4,748	403,452
	1927	7,487	51,837	659,535	100,244	68,219	419,972	185,312	1,492,606	1,163,844	3,600	415,582
	1928	6,945	48,281	656,679	89,801	61,751	418,535	178,332	1,459,324	1,153,540	3,749	453,364
	1929	6,726	51,430	637,117	104,205	63,944	440,377	187,173	1,498,972	1,127,758	4,341	440,733
	1930	4,913	40,646	579,374	100,290	71,819	454,747	176,947	1,428,945	1,060,706	3,761	410,087
	1931	4,100	46,631	538,323	98,199	111,031	443,007	170,325	1,411,036	1,002,945	3,041	357,587
	1932	3,484	40,270	479,208	74,128	82,282	409,270	170,086	1,259,637	890,493	2,427	369,809
	1933	4,070	32,486	492,524	69,159	70,120	416,414	174,421	1,259,104	890,601	2,027	396,057
Bedminster ..		No Goods Traffic dealt with.										

* Not available. † Including Telegraph Staff and Expenses from 1928. ‡ G.W. and L.M. & S. Joint—but only G.W. staff & traffic are given. § Includes Staff & Paybills for Stapleton Road prior to 1932. ¶ Staff and Paybills for Stapleton Road and Lawrence Hill included with Temple Meads after 1931.

Opposite:
Traffic dealt with at GWR Bristol stations, 1903–33.

Opposite below:
'Hymek' No D7000 passes through Parson Street with a Down goods, 1 June 1966. The road is set to take it into the goods loop at West Depot. *Author*

Left:
Class 9F 2-10-0 No 92242 seen at Narroways Hill Junction with a train of empty wagons. *W. H. Harbor/Author's collection*

Below left:
Westerleigh yard from the south, 21 April 1960. The photographer was standing on the site of the future M4. *Author*

Below:
No 03382 shunting at Lawrence Hill on 21 August 1980. The former Midland main line ran on the bridge and embankment in the background. *Author*

the closure of the Somerset & Dorset line on 6 March 1966, all coal traffic from Radstock was carried over the former BNSR line, but an unusually violent rainstorm on 10 July 1968 washed away part of the embankment north of Pensford station and, as it was uneconomic to repair this slip, coal traffic to Portishead power station and Imperial Smelting Processes Ltd (now Britannia Zinc) was diverted via Frome until the final colliery closed on 19 November 1973.

Goods trains came to Bristol from many parts of the country. The 1.30am Old Oak Common–Stoke Gifford was known as 'Long Tom' because it often consisted of 100 wagons, while the 5.10am Avonmouth–Weymouth was one of five animal feeding stuff trains which left Avonmouth between midnight and 6am. The 2.25pm Paddington–Temple Meads, known as the 'Paddy Mail' called at all stations and arrived at 10pm with a load of anything from two to 22 vans and hauled by any tender engine up to a 'King'. Its return working, known as the 'Cocoa' began in 1905 as the first GWR vacuum brake fitted goods train. *Circa* 1914 it was often worked by Pacific No 111 *The Great Bear* which hauled 70 wagons from East Depot to Acton in 3hr 5min. In the 1920s, 15 trains left Temple Meads goods depot between 5pm and 2.30am; seven were through trains running to such places as Birkenhead, Birmingham, Manchester, London, Carmarthen and Weymouth, while others were transfer trips connecting with through trains starting from the marshalling yards of East Depot, West Depot and Stoke Gifford.

The principal freight-only line was the Bristol Harbour Railway. Built by the GWR, B&E and Bristol Corporation, it was the first line to serve the city docks. Although only ³/₄mile in length, construction was difficult and expensive as a long viaduct and three bridges were needed. Making the line required the demolition of a vicarage, while cutting the 282yd-long tunnel involved the removal and reburial at Brislington of many bodies; the railway, of course, paying for the new burial ground. Bathurst Basin had to be crossed by an opening bascule bridge. Designed by Charles Richardson, who was to become chief engineer to the Severn Tunnel, it was powered by a steam engine now in the Bristol Industrial Museum. Although not fully completed, the works were sufficiently ready for a single mixed gauge line to open on 11 March 1872, although at that

Left:
Ivatt Class 2 2-6-2Ts Nos 41202 and 41203 at Ashton Bridge Junction with the RCTS special on 28 April 1957. Passenger trains did not normally use this line.
Author's collection

Below left:
Ex-Port of Bristol Authority No 30 Hudswell, Clarke (Works No D1171) at the Western Fuel Co's depot, Wapping, 18 August 1980.
Author

Above right:
'57xx' class 0-6-0PT No 3643 on arrival from Wapping Wharf. The Ashton Bridge signalman stands to collect the token on 6 June 1962.
E. T. Gill/Revd Brian Arman collection

Below right:
Ashton Swing Bridge c1905: rail on the lower deck and road on the upper. The control cabin is above.
Author's collection

date, neither of the two owning companies had any standard gauge lines in the city. Soon after opening, a $^1/_2$-mile-long extension was made to Wapping Wharf where the GWR gained berthing rights for a length of 1,600ft. This railway extension opened on 12 June 1876 and developed extensive grain traffic and also a large traffic principally comprising coal, timber and flour. When the main GWR line was blocked between Temple Meads and Parson Street for widening purposes on Sundays 26 April and 15 November 1931 for the demolition of two overline bridges, on both occasions passenger trains were diverted via the Harbour line, Ashton Swing Bridge and West Loop. With the rundown of the city docks, the line fell into disuse and was closed east of Wapping Wharf from 11 January 1964 and the track, viaduct and bridges subsequently dismantled. Ashton Meadows–Wapping Wharf remained for the daily coal train to the Western Fuel Co's depot. Under an agreement of 26 August 1977 the company worked wagons from Ashton Meadows using its Hudswell, Clarke 0-6-0, ex-PBA No D1171. The last train ran on 1 May 1987. The Bristol Industrial Museum has gained running rights over this section and from 1996 operates steam-hauled passenger trains.

In order to reduce carting and barging, under the Bristol Harbour Lines Act of 1897 the GWR obtained powers to connect the Harbour Railway with the Portishead branch and build an extension to Canon's Marsh on the north side of the Floating Harbour. Canon's Marsh, although close to the city docks, had not been developed because of lack of communication. The GWR also planned to use Canon's Marsh to deal with all West of England goods to and from Bristol and so reduce congestion at Temple Meads and Pylle Hill. The most interesting feature of the branch was Ashton Swing Bridge carrying the line over the New Cut. The bridge had two decks, the upper carrying a public road and the lower a double track railway. It was constructed by John Lysaght & Co Ltd for £70,389. The swing span weighed 1,000 tons, was 202ft 6in long and could turn either up or down stream. The bridge was worked by hydraulic power, the two three-throw reversible engines being situated in a control cabin above the roadway. Two vertical shafts turned the span, only one engine being required, the other acting as standby. The bridge was interlocked with GWR signalboxes on either side. The bridge, not swung since 1936, was made a permanent fixture in 1953. The control cabin and road deck were subsequently removed when a new road system was constructed in the area.

The line to Canon's Marsh led to the development of the district. The gas-works had direct rail communication, a chocolate factory was built and a lead pipe and sheet factory rebuilt and extended, while a marble and slate importer set up an establishment. Lairage, cattle pens and sidings were provided chiefly for Irish traffic, Cork and Waterford steamers discharging within a few yards and obviating a drive of a mile or two through the city to reach the railway. Rail access was provided to a foreign animals' wharf at Merchants' Dock. The 22 sidings in the yard could accommodate 531 wagons. In 1914, 115 men were employed at the depot and about 500 wagons exchanged daily, one engine shunting for 22hr daily and another for 8hr. Transfer trips were worked to various marshalling yards on the periphery of Bristol. The line from Ashton Swing Bridge Junction signalbox to Canon's Marsh closed on 14 June 1965.

Above:
'57xx' class 0-6-0PT No 3643 proceeds along Hotwell Road to Canon's Marsh, 13 January 1965.
Paul Strong

Right:
No D6351 near Cumberland Basin with a train from Canon's Marsh, 20 November 1963.
E. T. Gill/Revd Brian Arman collection

Above:
Bristol East Depot: Engineer's sidings, left, with permanent way yard beyond; the development on the right covers the site of the former Up yard. The HST is the 10.20 Temple Meads–Paddington on 17 March 1990.
Author

Right:
'57xx' class 0-6-0PT No 4603 with a goods train from Canon's Marsh passes Ashton Gate platform, 15 June 1960.
E. T. Gill/Revd Brian Arman collection

Opening the Severn Tunnel to goods traffic on 1 September 1886 had its influence on Bristol, causing additional congestion in the area as the Avoiding line via Badminton had yet to be built. Nine goods and mineral trains ran each way daily. To cope with the extra traffic passing through the Severn Tunnel, Up and Down yards at Bristol East Depot were opened in 1890 immediately west of Bristol (or St Anne's) No 1 Tunnel, the Up sidings being converted to a more economical gravitational yard on 7 October 1923. As rearranged, the yard consisted of 17 sidings. The first three were reception sidings to accommodate up to 131 wagons from trains waiting to be broken up by the hump shunting engine, while the remaining 14 roads were directly connected to the hump and held a total of 468 wagons. The Up yard dealt with 41 trains every 24hr involving passing an average of 1,300 wagons daily over the hump. The hump saved the cost of about 100 engine hours weekly. The shunter in charge of the ground frame was able to communicate with the shunting engine driver by means of a Klaxon: one blast indicating 'go

Continued on page 64

Opposite:
Bristol West Depot seen from Bedminster Down Road bridge on 21 August 1980. *Author*

Opposite below:
No 59104 near Hallen with a stone train for the second Severn crossing, 17 February 1994. *Author*

Left:
The Freightliner Depot with a Royal Mail container just loaded on the furthest wagon by crane on hire from Sparrow Ltd, 29 July 1980. *Author*

Below:
No 31217 heads an Up nuclear flask train with barrier wagons fore and aft and with a brake van at the rear on 16 June 1988. *Author*

ahead', two 'come back', three 'stop' and six 'obstruction danger'. Both yards at the East Depot closed 7 August 1967, the Up side becoming a Catchment Area Focal Point to which runnable crippled wagons were consigned, and the Down side, the Civil Engineer's yard. All these sidings are now closed and from 1994 Engineer's trains have been formed at Newport or Swindon.

On the other side of the city, West Depot opened in 1906 accommodating about 400 wagons plus storage for about a further 120 at Ashton Meadows sidings. The Down yard closed in the autumn of 1968 and was subsequently used for storing wagons and coaches. Part of the Up yard became a Freightliner Depot in 1974, through services being run to and from Manchester and Glasgow. The depot closed in May 1992, but at the time of writing the track is still *in situ*.

In 1903, conjointly with the opening of the Badminton line, a yard at Stoke Gifford was provided to cope mainly with Avonmouth traffic. Sidings were lengthened and an additional one laid in 1918 making a total of 14 roads in the Up yard and 10 in the Down. Both yards closed on 4 October 1971, much of the site being used for Bristol Parkway station and its adjoining car park.

Kingsland Road depot with 23 roads on the south side of the line just east of Temple Meads was a 'full loads' depot. In 1970 it employed 40 men including 26 NCL motor drivers, but 10 years later the number had fallen to nine including two drivers. Today most of the sidings have been lifted, a few remaining for Res use.

At one time about 60 wagons of coal were unloaded daily for the nearby gasworks. The yard also dealt with livestock except that to and from the West of England which was sorted at Pylle Hill, the former B&E goods depot. Pylle Hill, now reduced in size, is used by Res. The GWR built six storage sheds there for imported foodstuffs awaiting delivery. Lawrence Hill

Continued on page 67

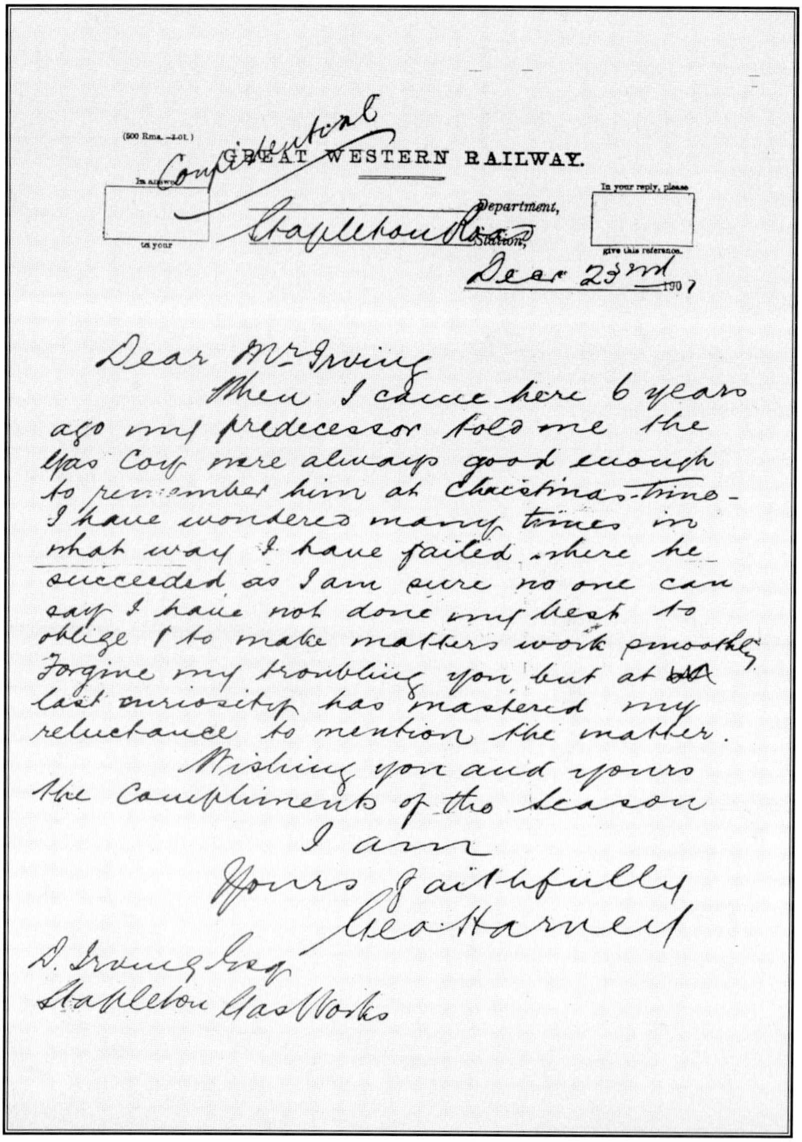

Confidential

(500 Rms.—1.01.)

GREAT WESTERN RAILWAY.

In answer to your

Stapleton Road Department, Station,

In your reply, please give this reference.

Dec 23rd 1907

Dear Mr Irving

When I came here 6 years ago my predecessor told me the Gas Coy were always good enough to remember him at Christmas-time - I have wondered many times in what way I have failed where he succeeded as I am sure no one can say I have not done my best to oblige & to make matters work smoothly. Forgive my troubling you but at last curiosity has mastered my reluctance to mention the matter.

Wishing you and yours the Compliments of the Season

I am

Yours faithfully

Geo Harvey

D. Irving Esq

Stapleton Gas Works

Left:
George Harvey's goods agent at Stapleton Road station, letter to D. Irving at Stapleton Gas Works asking for Christmas box, 23 December 1907. *Hugh Ballantyne collection*

Above right:
Avonside Wharf *c*1897. The GWR Temple Meads 'B' overhead signalbox can be seen on the far right. It opened in 1876 and closed *c*1898. *Author's collection*

Below right:
No 37203 and another member of the class, draw out of Stoke Gifford Yard with a train of roadstone wagons, 2 April 1984. Parkway station and its extensive car park can be seen beyond. *Hugh Ballantyne*

RAILWAY
6
RAILWAY
7

BRISTOL.

J. C. WALL,

APPOINTED AGENT

TO THE

Great Western & Bristol & Exeter

RAILWAY COMPANIES.

GOODS AND PARCELS.

FROM	SHOULD BE SENT TO
HIGH STREET CORN STREET CLARE STREET BROAD STREET SMALL STREET EXCHANGE EXCHANGE MARKETS	THE Universal PARCEL OFFICE, High Street.
WINE STREETT CASTLE STREET DOLPHIN STREET UNION STREET BRIDGE STREET MARYPORT STREET	THE BUSH OFFICE, Dolphin Street.
QUAYS NELSON STREET BROADMEAD MARSH STREET COLLEGE GREEN S. AUGUSTINE'S BACK DENMARK STREET THUNDERBOLT ST. KING STREET WELSH BACK QUEEN SQUARE BALDWIN STREET	THE ASSEMBLY ROOMS, OFFICE, Fronting the Quays AND Prince Street.
REDLAND COTHAM	Elephant and Castle, Redland.

FROM	SHOULD BE SENT TO
HOTWELLS CUMBERLAND BASIN ST. VINCENT PARADE GRANBY HILL	RAILWAY OFFICE, OPPOSITE Trinity Church, HOTWELLS.
QUEEN'S ROAD PARK STREET, &c., &c.	Railway Office, QUEEN'S ROAD, TOP OF PARK STREET.
MAUDLIN STREET ST. MICHAELS's HILL HORFIELD ROAD KINGSDOWN COTHAM	Portland Street, KINGSDOWN.
OLD MARKET STREET WEST STREET LOWER CASTLE ST.	THE White Hart Hotel, OLD MARKET STREET.
THOMAS STREET REDCLIFF STREET REDCLIFF HILL PHIPPEN STREET	Railway Office & Wharf, 127, REDCLIFF STREET.
BEDMINSTER NEW CUT CORONATION ROAD	THE Apple Tree Inn, BEDMINSTER.
CLIFTON	5, Clifton Place, NELSON PLACE.

N.B.—No Charge for Booking.

PARCELS are forwarded by EVERY Passenger Train from the BUSH OFFICE, DOLPHIN STREET, and from the UNIVERSAL OFFICE, HIGH STREET; and from the other Offices FOUR TIMES DAILY.

Goods Carted to or from any part of Bristol.

Furniture Removed to and from all parts of the Kingdom.

Warehouses for Storing Goods and Furniture on moderate terms.

SALE OF EXCURSION TICKETS.

FOR the better convenience of the Public, and by appointment of the Great Western Railway Company, EXCURSION TICKETS may now be obtained at the

Universal Parcels Office and City Cloak Room, Top of High Street,

BRISTOL.

FROM THE M. J. TOZER COLLECTION

Left:
Handbill issued by J. C. Wall, parcel agent at Bristol to GWR and B&E.
M. J. Tozer collection

Below:
No 60033 *Anthony Ashley Cooper* makes the first trip into the new Murco oil terminal at Westerleigh to test clearances. The M4 is in the background, 1 March 1991. *Author*

Opposite:
Warehouses at Avonmouth Dock *c* 1905.
Author's collection

and Stapleton Road, both now closed to goods, were for general goods, coal and other minerals. St Philip's Marsh mileage depot opened in April 1893 and closed on 3 September 1973, while in 1965 some sidings at Filton Junction were lifted and the remainder sold to a coal concentration depot. The 20–50 wagons dealt with daily were shunted by the Bristol Mechanised Coal Co's locomotive. Rail traffic ceased in December 1992.

The MR's Avonside goods depot had an extensive frontage on the Floating Harbour with warehouses for the storage of flour, grain, cheese, sugar, tinned foods, dried fruit and other merchandise. The company maintained a fleet of 19 120-ton barges for use to and from the warehouses at the city docks and for taking on goods from the sides of ships in order to convey them to Avonside for transfer to store or truck. A covered dock 160ft by 50ft was provided at the wharf for transferring perishable traffic under cover. At the MR's King's Wharf, Redcliff Street, were cellars or caves hewn out of the red sandstone and used for the storage of up to 8,000 barrels of non-inflammable oils, wax, etc. Commodities were accepted for conveyance by barge to rail at Avonside in precisely the same manner as at stations; electric, steam and hydraulic cranes there quickly loaded or discharged barges into or out of railway trucks. When most of the former Midland line out of Bristol closed on 1 February 1970, a new chord line was opened from Lawrence Hill to give access to the wharf, latterly used for cement and molasses, but Avonside finally closed in 1987. The northern end of the line is used on weekdays by a train to the refuse transfer station built on the site of the MR's Barrow Road cattle pens and carriage shed. The reception hall receives about 650 tonnes of waste from collection vehicles daily. Here the waste is compacted and placed in closed containers on 17 wagons to be sent to a landfill site at Calvert, Buckinghamshire, saving 19,000 lorry trips annually. On arrival of a train at Barrow Road the empty containers are removed and replaced by 17 full ones. The first train left on 18 November 1985.

To ease pressure on Barrow Road, and also Bath,

the MR opened a marshalling yard at Westerleigh in 1900/1. It had 13 Up and 12 Down roads. This yard closed on 19 January 1965. Part of the site was redeveloped 20 years later as the county council's Westerleigh Refuse Terminal where the binliner train calls *en route* to Calvert. On 1 March 1991 another part of the site was opened as Murco Petroleum's oil distribution depot. Products arrive in 100-tonne rail tankers and the depot is capable of handling up to 32. As a fire precaution, after pushing the wagons into the compound, the locomotive waits outside before collecting them after discharge.

In 1851 two Quakers, Albert Fry and John Fowler, established themselves as agricultural implement manufacturers and wheelwrights. Fowler left and later set up his famous firm at Leeds. Albert's cousin Theodore took the vacant partnership, their products including furniture vans designed to fit on railway wagons. In 1866 Theodore left and the Bristol Wagon Works Co Ltd was formed to take over the business, with Albert Fry as managing director. With the object of expanding business by building railway rolling stock, a new factory was built at Lawrence Hill beside the MR, a private siding leading to the works. In 1889, when it employed about 1,000 men, the firm became the Bristol Wagon

Above:
Great Western Refuse Transfer Station at Barrow Road on the site of the MR goods yard. This view, 17 March 1990, is towards Avon Wharf. *Author*

Left:
Port of Bristol Authority's No S11 *Bristol* built by Peckett, shunting at Avonmouth Docks, 13 January 1965. *Paul Strong*

Right:
'57xx' class 0-6-0PT No 3643 shunting at Temple Meads in 1951. The goods depot is in the background. *W. H. Harbor/Author's collection*

Below:
Dougal, Drewry Works No 2251, at Filton Coal Concentration depot on 20 August 1990. *Author*

& Carriage Works Co Ltd. Although some of its products were purchased by British railways, most were exported. Coach bodies were built for Taff Vale and Great Northern steam railmotors, some of the power units being supplied by the Avonside Engine Co. During World War 1 the company concentrated entirely on producing military material including rolling stock for railways in France and narrow gauge trench lines. In 1920 the company was purchased by Leeds Forge Co Ltd and the Newlay Wheel Co Ltd, but in 1923 Cammell, Laird Co Ltd took over the Leeds company and closed the Bristol works, the 13-acre site being bought by the Bristol Tramways & Carriage Co Ltd which it established as a central bus overhaul works.

Above:
2-8-2T No 7209 viewed at Narroways Hill Junction with a train of empty wagons.
W. H. Harbor/Author's collection

THE MOTIVE POWER SCENE

The first locomotive to enter Bristol did so in 1835, five years before the GWR arrived in the city. Details are vague, but it was a small engine and the colliery proprietors said that they were trying to make do until '...we can get some proper sized steam carriages on the Rail Road similar to those in use at the Welsh Collieries, Iron Works and elsewhere'. A letter in the Ashton Court Collection written by Sir John Smyth to E. F. Colston on 23 February 1835 explained that following a modification to increase its speed so that it could make two daily trips instead of one over the Bristol & Gloucestershire line, Bond & Winwood's steam carriage exploded, sending parts 300yd distant. Its steam was 'generated in tubes, not in the boiler, to render it more safe'.

When the line was taken over by the Bristol & Gloucester Railway, the tender of a Bristol firm, Stothert, Slaughter & Co, was accepted to work seven trains each way for £18,500 annually. In addition to providing the locomotives and rolling stock, the company also maintained the line. This meant that the BGR avoided an outlay for repair shops, carriage sheds, engine sheds and coke ovens. The locomotives built by Stothert, Slaughter & Co were of a design obtained from Bury, Curtis & Kennedy of Liverpool. They were 2-2-2s with inside bar frames, D-shaped fireboxes and weighed 18 tons in working order. No 7 *Wickwar*, as MR No 463, (the MR had purchased the stud from Messrs Stothert in July 1845) was wrecked when its boiler exploded on 8 January 1853, but the others made redundant when the MR converted to standard gauge. They were sold to Thomas Brassey in 1855/7 and used by him, and later the LSWR, on the broad gauge North Devon Railway. For working BGR goods traffic, Stothert & Co built two 0-6-0s and three 2-4-0s. Locomotive running costs worked out at 11½d a mile, the same as the GWR, but the GWR ran heavier trains. J. E. McConnell, the Birmingham & Bristol locomotive superintendent, giving evidence before the

Above:
MR No 413 and 2-4-0 viewed at Temple Meads after arriving with a Down train. *Author's collection*

Gauge Commission, said that one of Slaughter's largest goods engines, with the assistance of a pilot engine up the incline to Staple Hill, hauled a gross load of 235 tons and covered the 37½ miles to Gloucester in 4hr 13min including four stops. In 1846 Sharp Bros were given the contract to build a broad gauge engine for £3,000. In April 1847 Matthew Kirtley who had taken over the Locomotive Department, changed the order to four standard gauge 2-2-2 engines at £2,130 each and four tenders at £480. He instructed Sharp's to build them convertible and they were the first convertible engines ever built. They were standard gauge engines with long axles, and at first, while being used on the broad gauge, the wheels were outside the axleboxes. When the standard gauge was completed on 29 May 1854 their axles were shortened, the wheels placed inside the double frame and they were back on the road within 24hr. From this date, standard Midland engines were also able to use the line.

No express locomotives were stabled at Bristol until the turn of the century, principal trains being worked by Derby and Saltley sheds (mainly the latter). From 1854 until 1870 Kirtley 6ft 8in 2-2-2s Nos 120–9 worked expresses from Bristol to Birmingham when, as a result of enginemen sending a deputation to Kirtley complaining that singles were incapable of working heavy trains over the steeply-graded line, they were replaced by 2-4-0s Nos 820–9. In turn these were succeeded in 1880 by Johnson '1282' class 2-4-0s, Nos 1282–96 still working the line in 1919. In 1892 4-2-2 singles worked Derby–Bristol but were replaced by 4-4-0s a few years later, though until the mid-1920s could still be seen as train engines on relief as well as in use as pilots. Nos 673–9 ended their days on locals to Gloucester. The 4-4-0 Compounds and the '990' class did not penetrate to Bristol before the Grouping and the heaviest duties on the 'Devonian'

Top:
No 5038 *Morlais Castle* backs on to a Paddington express at Temple Meads on 17 June 1951.
Pursey Short

Above:
Compound No 1048 arrived at Temple Meads in August 1936 with a Down express.
M. J. Tozer collection

Above:
Ex-LMS No 46237 *City of Bristol* pictured at Temple Meads having worked the Down 11.15am 'Merchant Venturer' on trial against the 'Kings'. It returned to Paddington on the 4.15pm and carried out this turn for the next two days, 21 April 1955. *Revd Alan Newman*

Left:
'Jubilee' class 4-6-0 No 45663 *Jervis* seen at Temple Meads on a train from Birmingham on 22 August 1953. Diesel No W36 leaves with an intermediate trailer and No W35 at the rear. No W36 was later to be destroyed by fire at St Anne's Park, 10 April 1965. *R. E. Toop*

and Newcastle mail were performed by Class 3 4-4-0s, while lighter expresses were handled by those of Class 2. Compounds appeared in 1924, the post-Grouping series being run in on Derby–Bristol expresses and shortly after this Nos 1028–32 were shedded at Bristol. 'Jubilees' appeared in 1934 and gradually took over the heaviest trains, while during World War 2, 'Patriots', the first of which had appeared on the line in 1931, were given the heaviest train, the 7.40am from Bristol, always of 15 bogies. Class 5s did excellent work on Derby expresses handling 12-coach trains, while several Caprotti 'Black Fives' worked to Derby but although free runners they never had the 'guts' of piston valve engines when getting way from a stop or climbing. 'Crabs' were used on passenger trains and 'Royal Scot' No 46120 *Royal Inniskilling Fusilier* appeared in February 1949. In 1941 rebuilt SER 'F1' class 4-4-0s worked trains from Bristol to Gloucester, while in November 1941 the SR lent Drummond 'K10' mixed traffic 4-4-0s Nos 135 and 137–8 and 388–9 to the LMS, Nos 137–8 being shedded at Gloucester and Nos 135, 388/9 at Bristol. No 135 tended to work the Thornbury goods while Nos 388–9 shunted or worked local goods. They returned to the SR by March 1945. Eastern Region 'B1' 4-6-0s came in 1958 being seen especially on the 12.48pm from York, this train producing 'V2' 2-6-2 No 60954 on 16 November 1959. In January 1963 'V2' No 60945 arrived, but someone realised this type was not cleared for the route and so it returned via Didcot on the night freight to Woodford Halse. Eastern Region engines of the 'K1', 'K3', '01' and '04' classes are also recorded as having visited the Bristol area. LMS engines worked through to Weston-super-Mare on pre-World War 2 excursions from the Midlands, while in the latter days of steam, ER 'B1s' worked through Weston-super-Mare–Sheffield trains on Saturdays.

At the turn of the century 0-4-4Ts Nos 1274-81 were shedded at Bristol to work Clifton Down and Bath trains, from the 1930s being assisted by a Class 3P 2-6-2T. During 1947 Johnson 0-4-4Ts were mainly replaced by Stanier 2P 0-4-4Ts, only to be ousted two years later by Ivatt Class 2MTs of the '412xx' series aided by BR Standard Class 3MTs of the same wheel arrangement. On 19 February 1953 ex-GWR diesel railcar No W37, coach No 6582 and No W38 ran from Bristol to Bath Green Park on a gauging trip. From the beginning of the winter timetable, single and twin railcars worked some trains to Bath Green Park and, when unavailable, ex-GWR 2-6-2Ts or Panniers took over the same roster. 'Westerns', 'Peaks', 'Hymeks' and 'Warships' also

Left:
'Star' class 4-6-0 No 4021 *British Monarch* at the east end of Temple Meads during the summer of 1934. On the left is 'Saint' class No 2954 *Tockenham Court. E. J. M. Hayward*

Right:
Class 5 4-6-0 No 44853 pictured at Temple Meads with an up LMR express. No 44853 carries a 20A Leeds (Holbeck) shed plate. *W. H. Harbor/Author's collection*

Right:
Timetable of diesel railcar services from Bristol, *c*1937.

appeared on trains to Green Park, though BR DMUs were extremely rare.

Until the appearance of the Stanier '8Fs', goods trains were worked by 0-6-0s including the Avonmouth–London banana trains via Broom Junction and the Stratford-on-Avon & Midland Junction line. Somerset & Dorset 2-8-0s worked freight trains from Avonmouth and Westerleigh to Bath, while the occasional Beyer-Garratt or LNWR 0-8-0 put in an appearance on trains from the north. From March 1950 a Garratt from Toton worked daily to Westerleigh, spent the night at Barrow Road and returned with the early morning freight or empties the next day. In 1954 ex-Barry Railway 0-6-2T GWR No 285, which had been withdrawn the previous year, was in use as a stationary boiler at Barrow Road. The sharply-curved Avonside Wharf line required MR 0-4-0STs and in post-Grouping years LYR 'Pugs' put in an appearance. In 1961 the duties of Nos 51217–8 were taken over by 204hp diesel shunters Nos D2134–5, later classified as 03. The first diesel shunter on ex-LMS lines at Bristol was No 13187 which arrived at Barrow Road on 1 June 1958 and began work the following day.

For the opening of the GWR between Bristol and Bath on 31 August 1840, six of Daniel Gooch's new engines were ready: *Arrow* and *Dart* had been built at Bristol by Stothert, Slaughter & Co, while *Fire Ball*, *Spit Fire* and *Lynx* of the 'Firefly' class and *Meridian* of the 'Sun' class were made by various other manufacturers. *Meridian* was rumoured to have come in parts by barge and been assembled in Saltford Tunnel. The first engine shed, a parallelogram in shape, was

GWR STREAMLINED RAIL CAR SERVICES

ONE CLASS ONLY (LIMITED ACCOMMODATION) — MONDAYS TO FRIDAYS INCLUSIVE BETWEEN

BRISTOL, BATH, TROWBRIDGE, SALISBURY, YEOVIL & WEYMOUTH

	a.m.		p.m.	p.m.	p.m.		p.m.		p.m.	
BRISTOL (Temple Meads) dep.	8 10	..	12 25	..	12D40	..	2D45	..	..	..
BATH arr.	8 25	..	12 40	..	1D5	..	3D10	..	..	..
BATH dep.	8 26	..	12 42	..	1K7	..	3D12	..	..	..
BRADFORD-ON-AVON	—	..	—	..	1K30	..	3D43	..	..	..
TROWBRIDGE arr.	8 46	..	1 2	..	1K37	..	3D51	..	..	..
TROWBRIDGE dep.	8 47	..	1 3	..	1 55	..	3D52	..	..	..
WESTBURY arr.	8 54	..	1 10	..	2 2	..	3D59	..	..	..
WESTBURY dep.	8 55	..	1 12	..	2 4	..	4 10	..	..	..
WARMINSTER	—	..	1 20	..	—	..	—	..	..	..
SALISBURY arr.	—	..	1 45	..	—	..	—	..	..	..
FROME	9 4	..	..	..	2 12	..	4 20	..	..	..
CASTLE CARY	—	..	..	..	—	..	4 39	..	..	..
YEOVIL (Pen Mill) dep.	9 36	..	..	..	2 44	..	4 55	..	7 45	..
MAIDEN NEWTON	9 53	..	..	..	3 2	..	5 11	..	8 1	..
DORCHESTER	10 5	..	..	2 50	3 14	..	5 22	..	8 12	..
MONKTON CAME HALT (Golf Links)	—	..	..	2 54	3 17	..	—	..	—	..
UPWEY WISHING WELL HALT	—	..	..	2 59	3 21	..	—	..	—	..
UPWEY JUNCTION	—	..	..	3 2	3 24	..	—	..	—	..
RADIPOLE HALT	—	..	..	3 6	3 27	..	—	..	—	..
WEYMOUTH (Town) arr.	10 15	..	..	3 10	3 30	..	5 32	..	8 25	..
PORTLAND arr.	10D45	..	..	..	4D16	..	6D21	..	9E18	..

	a.m.	a.m.	p.m. 1st and 3rd Class	p.m.	p.m.	p.m. To Taunton (arrive 6.20 p.m.)	p.m. 1st and 3rd Class	p.m.	p.m. 1st and 3rd Class	p.m. From Taunton (depart 6.35 p.m.)	p.m. 1st and 3rd Class	p.m.
PORTLAND dep.	9D43	..				4D32		5D32		..		
WEYMOUTH (Town) dep.	10 10	11 0		..	..	5 0		6 5	6 15	..		..
DORCHESTER	10 21	11 12		..	..	—		6 16	6 34	..		..
MAIDEN NEWTON	10 32	11 24		..	..	—		6 27	6 56	..		..
YEOVIL (Pen Mill)	10 49	11 44		..	..	5 38	5 44	6 45	7 25	7 28		..
CASTLE CARY	11 6	—		..	..		6 10			—		..
FROME	—	12 16		..	..		6 36			7 58		..
SALISBURY	—	—		..	2 40		..			—	7 25	..
WARMINSTER dep.	—	—		..	3 6		..			—	7 58	..
WESTBURY arr.	11 24	12 25		..	3 15		6 45	..		8 7	8 6	..
WESTBURY dep.	[illegible]	..	[illegible]	[illegible]	3 25		6 55	..		..	8 14	8 20
TROWBRIDGE arr.	11 33	..	12 40	1 7	3 34		7 2	..		..	8 21	8 27
TROWBRIDGE dep.	11 34	..	12 50	..	..		7 15	..		..	8 24	8 28
BRADFORD-ON-AVON	—	..	12 59	..	..		7 23	..		..	8 32	8 37
FRESHFORD	—	..	1 6	..	..		7 30	..		..	—	8 42
LIMPLEY STOKE	—	..	1 9	..	..		7 33	..		..	—	8 47
BATHAMPTON	—	..	1 17	..	..	..	7 42	..		..	—	8 55
BATH arr.	11 53	..	1 21	..	..	..	7 46	..	..	..	8 47	8 59
BATH dep.	11 57	..	1 24	..	..	..	7 49	..	..	..	8 51	9 0
OLDFIELD PARK	—	..	1 27	..	..	..	7 52	..	..	..	—	9 3
SALTFORD	—	..	1 33	..	..	..	7 58	..	..	..	—	9 8
KEYNSHAM & S'M'RD'E	—	..	1 39	..	..	..	8 4	..	..	..	—	9 14
ST. ANNE'S PARK	—	..	1 44	..	..	..	8 10	..	..	..	—	9 20
BRISTOL (Temple Meads) arr.	12 15	..	1 48	..	..	..	8 18	..	..	..	9F 8	9 24

YEOVIL and TAUNTON

	p.m.
WEYMOUTH (Town)	5 0
YEOVIL (Pen Mill) dep.	5 45
TAUNTON arr.	6 20
MINEHEAD arr.	7D33
EXETER	7D 7
TORQUAY	8D10
PLYMOUTH (North Road)	8D42

	p.m.
PENZANCE dep.	1D15
PLYMOUTH (NORTH ROAD)	4D10
TORQUAY	4D17
EXETER	5D40
ILFRACOMBE	3D10
TAUNTON dep.	6 35
YEOVIL Town	7 18
YEOVIL Pen Mill arr.	7 20
WEYMOUTH (Town) arr.	8 25

The 11.0 a.m. Weymouth to Dorchester (one class only) will start at 11.3 a.m. and run three minutes later Mondays to Fridays (inclusive).
The 3.10 p.m. Dorchester to Weymouth, one class only, will start at 2.50 p.m. and run 20 minutes *earlier* Mondays to Fridays (inclusive).
The 4.35 p.m. Yeovil (Pen Mill) to Weymouth (one class only) will leave Evershot at 5.11 p.m. and run 12 minutes later thence to Weymouth Mondays to Fridays (inclusive).
The 7.53 p.m. Frome to Westbury (one class only) will run 17 minutes later, Mondays to Fridays (inclusive).

D—1st & 3rd class. E—1st & 3rd class. On Wednesdays arrive 8.56 p.m. F—Bristol (Stapleton Rd.) K—1st and 3rd Class. Runs 5 minutes later on Thursdays.

NOTE. Services by Streamlined Rail Cars are shewn in heavy type.
For other Train Services in these Districts see Company's Time Tables.

a small three-road affair accommodating 15 locomotives and situated on the north side of the line near the site of the later South Wales Junction, while opposite were coke ovens with a weekly producing capacity of about 450 tons, supplying all GWR engines with smokeless fuel and superseding the original small establishment at West Drayton. Coking coal from the Rhondda Valley travelled by sea from Cardiff to Bristol, there being no rail communication at that date.

At first the B&E was worked by the GWR, but in 1849 its financial position was such that it became completely independent and had its own engines and rolling stock. Locomotive workshops opened at Bristol in January 1852 on the site of what became the Bath Road shed, were considerably extended in September 1854, turned out their first locomotive in 1859 and built 34 more during the next 16 years, the total comprising 23 broad gauge, 10 standard and two 3ft gauge. The B&E having a relatively short main line of only 76 miles, tended to use tank engines, the most impressive examples being 4-2-4 express tank locomotives with 9ft driving wheels, designed by James Pearson. 4-4-0STs were also used for main line passenger duties, other tank engines being of the 2-2-2T, 2-2-2WT, 0-6-0ST and 0-4-0WT wheel arrangements, the latter designed for shunting. Tender engines comprised those of the 4-2-2, 0-6-0 and 2-4-0 types.

Practically all classes of GWR engines have appeared at Bristol, including the de Glehn Atlantics. *Circa* 1905 *La France* left Exeter with 12 corridor

Opposite above:
Gas turbine No 18000 enters Temple Meads with a train from Paddington *c*1952.
S. Miles Davey, courtesy P. G. Davey

Opposite below:
Nos W51505/E53617, of set No C983, leave Temple Meads on 16 June 1988 with the 12.06 to Weymouth. *Author*

Above:
The driver oiling 'Star' class 4-6-0 No 4062 *Malmesbury Abbey* at Temple Meads, 1951. Observe the Bristol East colour light signals, and on the left-hand side of the gantry, a semaphore shunting signal to permit working in the Bristol Goods shunting neck.
W. H. Harbor/Author's collection

Above left:
'Jubilee' class 4-6-0 No 45658 *Keyes* comes off a north–west through passenger train on 8 July 1951. Bath Road shed is in the background.
Pursey Short

coaches — 330 tons behind the tender — ran 75$^1/_2$ miles to Bristol start-to-stop in 77$^1/_2$ min, then carried on to London with the same load, the 118$^1/_2$ miles taking 118min. Another interesting engine was Pacific No 111 *The Great Bear* whose weight limited it to the London–Bristol line on which it

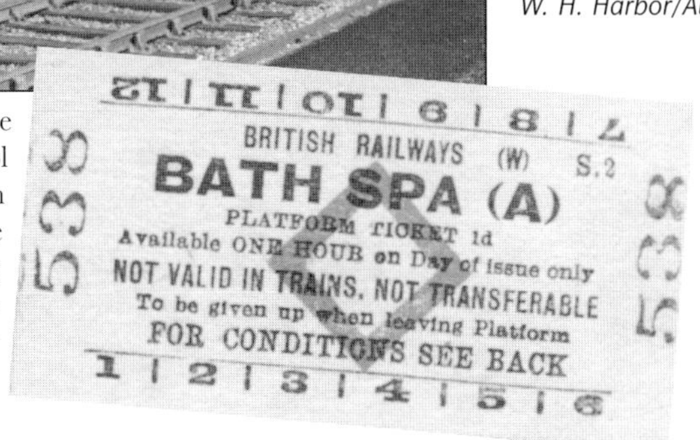

worked both expresses and fast fitted freights, the latter also being handled by 2-8-0s of the '47xx' class handling up to 70 vehicles. Tank engines too were used on this route and in 1907 it is recorded that the 5.30am newspaper and mail train from Paddington was worked to Bristol by a 4-4-2T equipped with water pick-up apparatus, arriving at 8.28, returning on the 9.35am from Bristol and arriving at Paddington at 12.20am. In 1911 a railmotor and trailer worked 14 trips each way between Temple Meads and Clifton Down, but were not used through Clifton Down Tunnel or on the Hotwells line. In the 1930s Drummond 'D15' 4-4-0s ran from Salisbury to Bristol and returned every evening, while for a later period 'U' class 2-6-0s worked through regularly on a weekday and returned on the 8.45pm Bristol–Eastleigh mail. Bulleid Pacifics were seen on postwar football specials. In 1934 some surplus 2-8-0Ts intended for working in South Wales, were converted to 2-8-2Ts carrying a larger bunker almost equalling the coal capacity of a tender engine, so that they could undertake main line coal traffic working; some were used between South Wales and Salisbury.

Between August 1940 and March 1941, 12 GWR engines were damaged in air raids on Bristol. During World War 2 trains of USA-built 2-8-0s passed through on their way to Swindon and after being checked over were seen on freights, as were GWR-built LMS '8Fs' and WD 'Austerities'. During this period local passenger services were worked by '45xx' 2-6-2Ts, Pannier tanks or diesel railcars. Gas turbine No 18000 made its appearance on Paddington trains in 1949, followed three years later by No 18100. The first BR Standard to appear was the 'Britannia' Class 4-6-0 and was followed by most of the other classes. BR DMUs were first used at Bristol on 18 August 1958 when two Gloucester Railway Carriage & Wagon Works, Nos W55018–9, were used on alternate days on the Clifton Extension line. By 3 September, the Bristol allocation of Derby-built suburban three-car units, later Class 116, began to arrive and

Left:
Body of No 43128 lifted at Bath Road depot, 29 June 1991. *Author*

Below left:
'Saint' class 4-6-0 No 2954 *Tockenham Court* at Pylle Hill Junction *en route* to Bath Road shed after hauling a partially vacuum-braked goods from Severn Tunnel Junction on 8 July 1951. *Pursey Short*

Above right:
'47xx' class 2-8-0 No 4702 pictured by the coaling stage, St Philip's Marsh, on 26 September 1937. Notice the heaps of ashes. *Author's collection*

Right:
No 5552 *Silver Jubilee* in black and chrome livery at Temple Meads, probably on 28 May 1935.
S. Miles Davey, courtesy P. G. Davey

Overleaf:
No 6928 *Underley Hall* and No 6876 *Kingsland Grange* in St Philip's Marsh shed, 6 February 1964.
Revd Alan Newman

these soon took over the training trips. The first stage of Bristol suburban dieselisation was introduced on 5 October 1958 and Stage Two came into force on 17 November. DMUs allocated to Bristol for the period ending December 1958 included 56 power cars. On 6 April 1959 stopping trains on the Swindon–Weston-super-Mare and Bristol–Westbury-Weymouth lines were dieselised. Later 'Warships', 'Westerns', 'Hymeks' and Class 47s appeared on expresses and in 1968/9 Paddington-Bristol was the hunting ground of Brush experimental No D0280 *Falcon*, which in the author's experience, could always be relied on to bring its train in on time.

Class 50s made redundant by London Midland Region's West Coast electrification superseded Class 47s and 'Westerns' on Bristol–Paddington trains on 6 May 1974. Many failures occurred initially because on Brunel's main line the locomotives were having to run at their full speed for longer than they had been required to do previously. Eventually matters were cured by altering the armatures and by 1978 the Western Region had succeeded in improving them to the reliability of Class 47s. Meanwhile, following trial runs between Bristol and London on 16–19 December 1974, HST No 252001 appeared on some trains in 1975, a regular service beginning in the spring of 1977. The HSTs proved a great success and within a few months of their introduction InterCity patronage rose by nearly 18%.

The Bristol Port Railway & Pier possessed only two locomotives, 0-4-2Ts of the Bury or Fairburn type whose early history is obscure; they were probably St Helen's Railway No 4 *Hercules* and No 23 *Hero* built in 1856 and 1853/4. On the BPRP they carried a livery of dark green and were not fitted with a vacuum brake. They were hauled to the line through the streets of Bristol by 30 MR horses. Small repairs were undertaken at the company's locomotive depot at Shirehampton, but were sent to Peckett's for more extensive work and a replacement engine was hired from the MR. 0-6-0WTs Nos 2002 and 2013 are known to have been borrowed and as the latter was being hauled on a cart along the newly-made Perry Road one Whit Saturday, it became embedded

6928

in soft ground and required 60 horses to drag it out. Fortunately it arrived in time for working the Bank Holiday Monday traffic. When the GWR and MR took over the line, the 0-4-2Ts were condemned and replaced with locomotives from GWR stock.

The first GWR locomotive shed at Bristol was on the north side of the line east of Temple Meads near the site of the later South Wales Junction and was a three-road shed, a four-road building being added subsequently. Bath Road shed (BRD in the GWR code, 82A until 1 May 1973, BR from May 1973) was originally a six-road B&E depot set diagonally beside the locomotive works. The complex was rebuilt in 1934 when lines either side of Temple Meads were quadrupled. The main shed, 210ft by 167ft, had 10 roads and was built approximately on the site of the locomotive works. It was constructed of bricks and had a slated roof with the usual raised central louvred and glazed vent to each bay. Beside it was a three-road repair shop, 170ft by 50ft, steel framed with brick walls and a slated roof, a coal stage surmounted by a 135,000gal water tank separating the two buildings. The water came from Fox's Wood pumping station which also supplied St Philip's Marsh shed as well as the water troughs. Originally lifted from the river by steam pump, an electric pump was fitted latterly, a bell ringing at Bath Road when a failure occurred. Fish were sometimes sucked through the 15in-diameter pipes, the author having it on good authority that an eel spent three years in the water tank of a shunting engine. On the east side of the Bath Road complex was a gasworks supplying fuel for lighting buildings and the yards. Gas was piped to Marsh Pond, Dr Day's and Malago Vale sidings for charging coaches, boys being employed to 'gas up' coaches and having to endure the smell clinging to their hands and clothes. Rail tank wagons were sent to stations in the area to replenish coach gas tanks. From 1934 when the LMS gasworks at Bristol closed, that company obtained its supply from the GWR. Bath Road shed closed to steam on 12 September 1960, the locomotives being transferred to St Philip's Marsh and Barrow Road.

The depot was rebuilt at a cost of over £700,000 and opened on 18 June 1962 as a diesel depot servicing about 140 diesels. It was of three sections:

1. A three-road running or 'daily' shed for fuelling and very light maintenance.
2. A light maintenance shed with six roads, used for more thorough examinations and for work which took too long to be satisfactorily undertaken in the running shed, where a locomotive stayed for only a short period.
3. A heavy lifting shop with overhead gantry crane and used for major repairs of locomotives and HST power cars.

By the shed is a 146-ton Rapier 65ft turntable

Opposite:
'Z' class 0-8-0T No 30952 with motion removed, near Barrow Road shed *en route* for the scrap yard, 17 January 1965.
E. T. Gill/Revd Brian Arman collection

Above:
'8F' class 2-8-0 No 48711, with Fowler-pattern tender, seen at Barrow Road on 30 June 1965. This engine was built by the SR at Brighton in 1944 and on completion first worked as LNER '06' class No 7657. Notice the upper lamp bracket in the more accessible position on the right of the smokebox door.
Revd Alan Newman

Above left:
The 32-tonne travelling crane outside St Philip's Marsh depot, 16 January 1996. *Author*

Below left:
BR Standard Class 5MT 4-6-0 No 73092 backs out of Temple Meads on 14 April 1962. *Author*

which was also part of an escape road from the shed to the Avoiding line and could be used if the main entrance became blocked. In the depot yard a 145-ton steam crane and 75-ton diesel crane were kept to cover the area Tiverton–Bromsgrove, Warminster and Didcot. Other equipment included two large snowploughs. As Res fuelling and examination work was transferred to Barton Hill and a 32-tonne overhead crane was installed at St Philip's Marsh capable of lifting power units and thus obviating the need to send power cars to Bath Road, the latter shed became redundant, lost its Class 47/8 allocation from 28 May 1995 and was mothballed on 22 September 1995.

St Philip's Marsh depot (SPM then 82B until June 1964) was opened on 9 July 1910 and basically supplied engines for freight working, while Bath Road concentrated on passenger engines. The Marsh did, however, provide power in the form of 'Halls' and 'Granges' for the many north to west trains using the Avoiding line, engines or crews being changed near the shed. Situated south of the Avoiding line, it was the second largest depot on the GWR. A total of 28 roads radiated from each of the two turntables. Adjacent was a two-road repair shop which later had a steel-framed corrugated extension for the maintenance of GWR diesel railcars by AEC fitters, GWR cleaners wiping the bodywork with cleaning oil. The main building, 246ft by 364ft, was of brick standing on concrete piles as it was on made ground. Below the water tank, which held 145,000gal, was a two-road coal stage. The manually-operated turntable used for larger engines was in the roundhouse furthest from the Avoiding line, while the electric turntable for smaller engines was in another building. The depot closed on 13 June 1964 when the few remaining engines were transferred to Barrow Road, the shed being demolished the following February and a wholesale fruit and vegetable market erected.

In 1949 '2021' class 0-6-0PTs were used on the Harbour lines and at Canon's Marsh, but were replaced by a modern edition — the '16xx' class. '66xx' class 0-6-2Ts were used on Stoke Gifford–Avonmouth transfer trips. BR Standard Class 9s and ex-LMS '8Fs' appeared at the Marsh in the late 1950s. The first diesel-electric shunter at Bristol was GWR No 2 which arrived in January

Left:
No 47811 awaits attention in the wheel profiling shop, St Philip's Marsh, on 16 January 1996. *Author*

Above:
No 37715 *British Petroleum* at Temple Meads, on 31 October 1995, running Up light engine. The Middle Siding East ground frame, opened 23 March 1970, is in the foreground. *Author*

Right:
Barton Hill Preventive Maintenance shed, 31 July 1980. The pit on the right was used by the 'Bristol Pullman'. The shed has since received cladding. *Author*

1949 as No 15100, the only GWR engine to be renumbered under the BR scheme; No 15107 arrived new in November. By February 1954 Nos 13000–3 had arrived and in September 1956 ex-Southern Region shunter No 15230 appeared. Twelve diesel shunters arrived at the Marsh in 1958 and displaced Pannier tank engines.

Barrow Road (MR code 8, LMS 22A, and BR 82E) was a brick-built roundhouse, but, unlike the GWR sheds, it had a modern coaling tower. In 1935 LMS motive power depots were reorganised into locomotive supply concentration and garage schemes, Bristol becoming a main or concentration depot, with Gloucester, Bath/Radstock, Templecombe, Highbridge, Tewkesbury and Wells as garage depots. The object of the scheme was to effect economies by reducing the necessity of stocking so many parts at smaller depots. The district locomotive superintendent had his office at Bristol. The depot was well-equipped with a wheel drop pit, wheel lathe, two sheer legs, an ash disposal plant and two turntables. It closed on 16 November 1965 but did not indicate the complete cessation of steam in Bristol because steam-hauled freight trains between Birmingham and Bristol continued until August 1966. However, by October Barrow Road shed was demolished.

The four-road Marsh Junction DMU depot (code

Continued on page 90

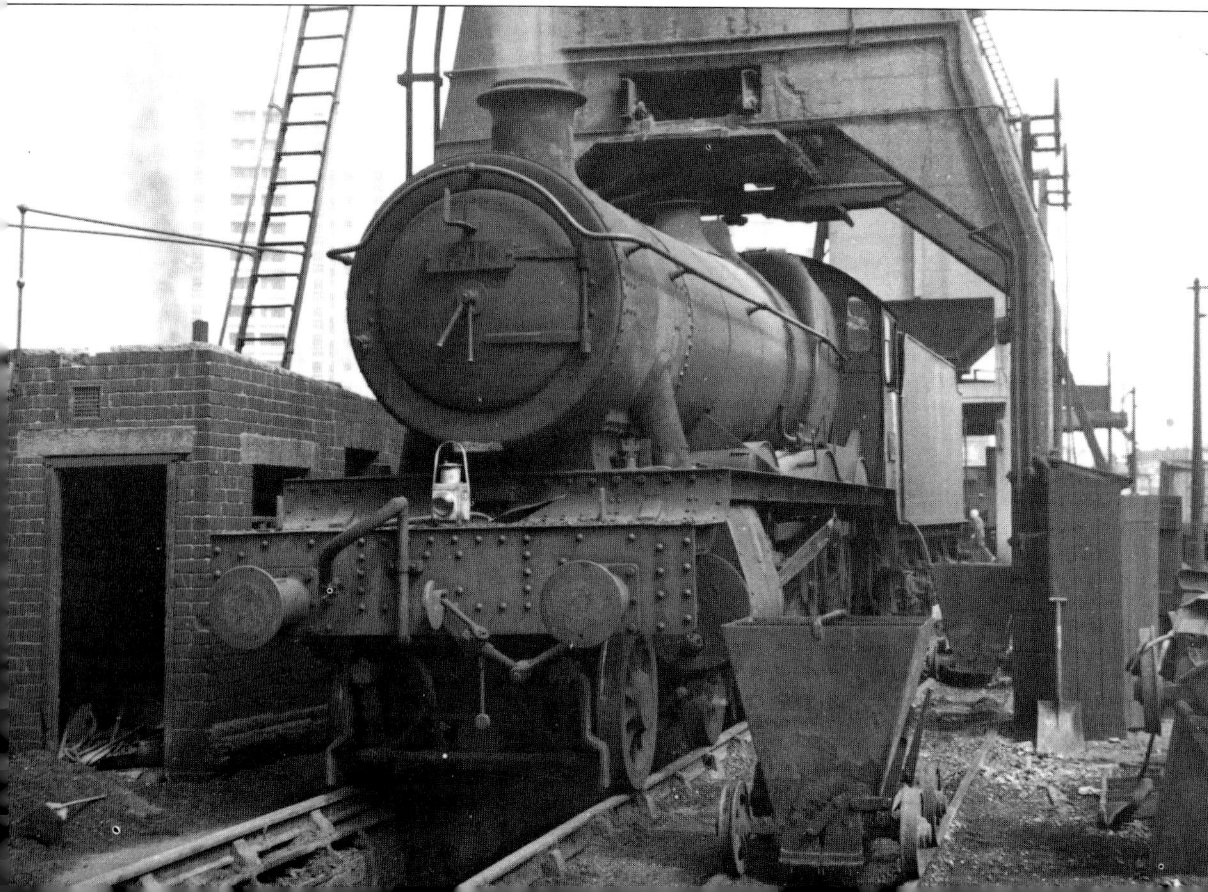

Above left:
No 7925 *Westol Hall* passes Barrow Road MPD with a train for the West of England. A Class 9F 2-10-0 stands below the ash plant and a Pannier tank near the coal tower on 24 July 1965.
E. T. Gill/Revd Brian Arman collection

Left:
On 14 May 1965 No 6910 *Gossington Hall* is seen below the ash-handling plant built of ferro-concrete, 1938/9. A narrow gauge ash wagon stands in the foreground. No 6910 has its name and smokebox number plate removed. Built in December 1940, it was withdrawn in October 1965. *Revd Alan Newman*

Top:
Three '57xx' class 0-6-0PTs in the Barrow Road roundhouse on 12 March 1965. Left to right: No 3696 with snowplough, No 9623 and No 9680. The turntable well is in the foreground.
Revd Alan Newman

Above:
Two engines at Barrow Road, their home shed, on 21 April 1955: Class 1F 0-6-0T No 41706 and Class OF 0-4-0ST No 51212. *Revd Alan Newman*

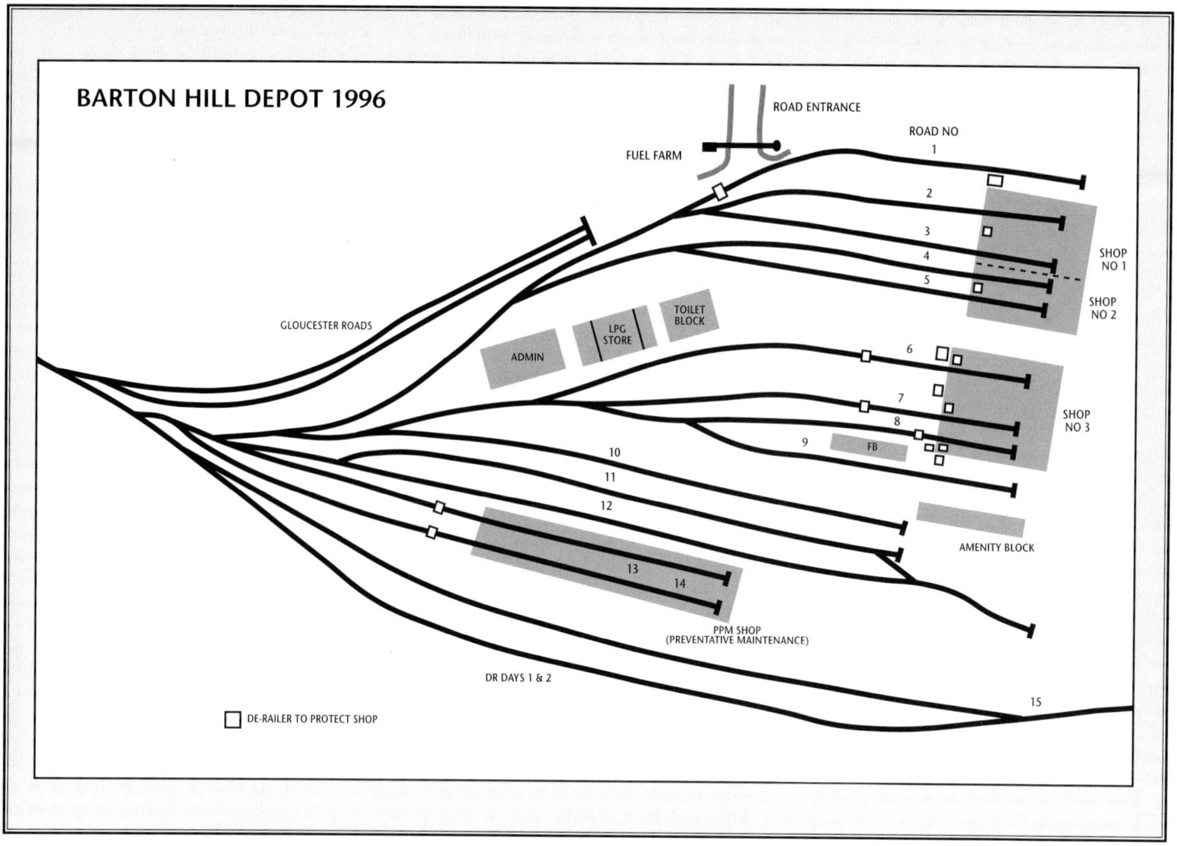

Above:
Plan of Barton Hill Depot, 1996.

Left:
Barton Hill stores: discs show which tools are out, 22 January 1996. *Author*

Above right:
An engine on each road at Bath Road shed, 7 June 1952.
R. E. Toop

Right:
No 6900 *Abney Hall* at Bath Road shed, 1951.
W. H. Harbor/Author's collection

BJ May 1973–December 1976 and PM subsequently) brought into use on 23 February 1959 also serviced 'D6xx' and 'D8xx' diesel-hydraulics until Bath Road reopened as a diesel depot. Marsh Junction's 1965 allocation was 32 cross–country trains, 12 suburban, four single cars and one Pullman set. It was closed on 18 May 1970 so that it could be used for maintaining the Chief Civil Engineer's plant, DMUs being maintained at Bath Road, but still fuelled at Marsh Junction. In the summer of 1973 when MkIID coaches were used on Bristol–London services, maintenance of their 1,000V electric heating had to be carried out under cover, Roads 3 and 4 of the former DMU depot being utilised for this and 1 and 2 for the maintenance of the CCE's yellow track machines. Today the building is also used for coach and van body repairs and the storage of Nos 37601–2 pending the inauguration of the EPS (European Passenger Services) service.

With the introduction of HSTs, Bath Road was unable to cope with the added workload of maintaining them, so a purpose-built shed was erected in 1974/5 by George Wimpey & Co at a cost of £1.5 million. The 700ft-long, three-road depot opened on the site of the former cattle pens in September 1975. Fluorescent strip lighting was used throughout the shed and the white floor was coated with a paint which resisted oil impregnation. This gave a light and clean appearance to the depot and encouraged staff to keep their footwear clean and not spread dirt through the trains. By the fuelling facilities, grids are placed in the floor to allow spillage to run through. The concept of the shed was that the entire HST unit could be serviced in one place at one time, whereas hitherto locomotives and coaches had been serviced in different places. Four Matterson 20-tonne SWL jacks lift a power car for the bogie changing or maintenance, the jacks being designed so that they can be moved round the shed by fork lift.

The three interior roads are lettered A, B and C,

Above:
Nos 47627 *City of Oxford*, 47634 *Henry Ford*, 31457 and 31431 at Bath Road shed on 16 June 1988, from the same viewpoint as the lower picture on page 89. *Author*

Right:
Avonside Engine Co Ltd trade card. *M. J. Tozer collection*

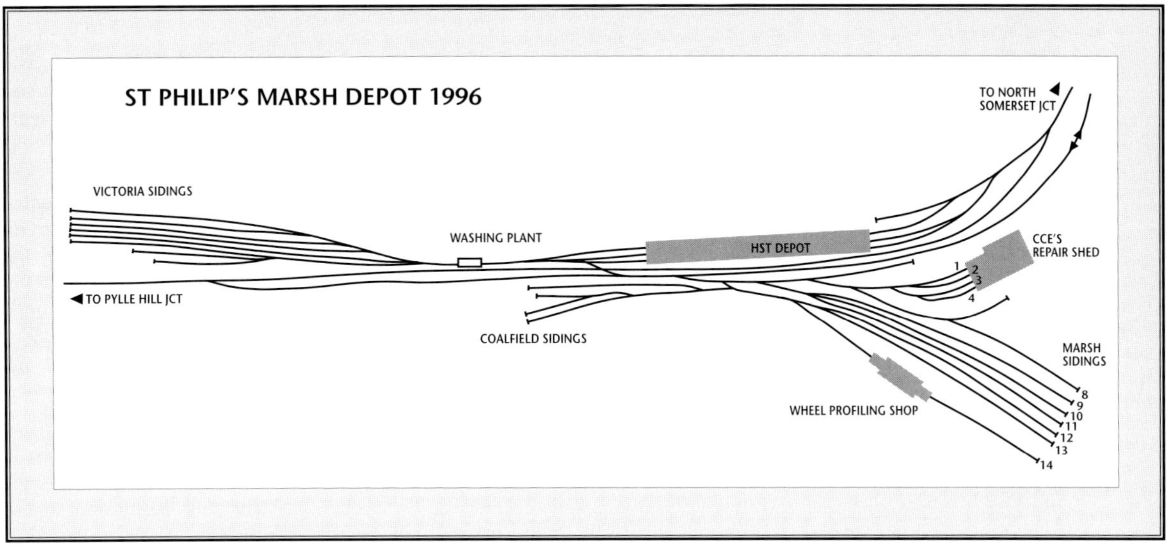

while D road is outside. Each road has fuelling, watering and topping up coolant facilities at each end where power cars stop, the facilities doubled at one end as Great Western HSTs have an extra first class coach making them 2+8, rather than the 2+7 of the Cross Country HSTs. In order to cater for the Great Western HSTs the depot had to be extended by one coach length. Cross Country HSTs tend to be sent to Leeds, Neville Hill for maintenance. St Philip's Marsh also maintains InterCity Great Western locomotives, mainly used on sleeper services.

Each HST set comes in nightly for maintenance and 'A' examinations carried out every 2–3 days depending on mileage. As 11–15 sets are dealt with each night, only the quicker jobs are tackled then, daytime fitters carrying out the longer examinations and if not completed by evening, the set has to be removed outside to make room for those arriving for daily maintenance. While within the depot building an HST is plugged into a shore supply to avoid its batteries being drained by air conditioning, lighting and refrigeration units. Following a set being serviced, it is taken through the Britannia carriage washing plant *en route* to stabling at Victoria Sidings on the site of the former St Philip's Marsh goods yard. At Victoria Sidings HSTs are plugged into a shore supply and have their interiors cleaned and the end exteriors which cannot be dealt with by the mechanical plant. Their toilet tanks are filled here with water, but drinking water is taken on at Temple Meads. Before removing a train from Victoria Sidings, a driver will walk round it checking oil and diesel oil levels, head and tail lights, windscreen wipers and soundness of doors.

Top:
Plan of St Philips Marsh Depot, 1996.

Above:
Marsh Junction sidings with wheel profiling shop right and Thames Turbo for wheel profiling in centre distance. 16 January 1996. *Author*

In 1991 a wheel profiling shop was built to carry out work on power cars, DMUs, locomotives and coaches. To keep its interior clean and fume-free, vehicles are moved in and out by capstan.

The area's wagon shops were at Barton Hill. Originally for the MR and GWR, they were set side by side, the intervening wall only being breached in 1962. In 1980 four sets of Yeoman tippler wagons arrived weekly for preventive maintenance (a total of 120 wagons) plus about 40 other wagons. The Dutch-barn-like Preventive Maintenance Shed was built in 1975 over two roads (the wall of the old broad gauge locomotive turntable pit being discovered when digging its foundations). One of the roads had an inspection pit built in 1958 for DMUs and later used by the 'Bristol Pullman'. The shops also repaired porters' barrows and platform seats. In later years the depot maintained Avon County Council rubbish container wagons.

Res has developed Barton Hill into a depot for maintaining its vans and locomotives. Numbered from west to east, the four buildings are the three stone buildings 1, 2, and 3 and the PPM (Planned Preventive Maintenance), the latter being the Dutch-barn shed now with walls of steel cladding. Early in 1996 work was being carried out in the ex-Bristol & Gloucester Railway buildings converting basically sound NEA vans to NBA. This involved blocking off windows and giving a van a new steel floor, roller doors, new lighting and new bogies. When working on van roofs, men wear a safety harness clipped to a wire slung below the shop roof. The vans are painted by hand with 50 microns of undercoat and 75 microns of topcoat. The carpenter's shop has been reduced in size as there are no longer timber-built wagons, its present use being mainly for repairs to doors and ladders. Using softwood was found to be a false economy and today hardwood is utilised. Maintenance work is eased by the fact that most Res vehicles are in four-vehicle sets (NBA, NKA, NKA, NBA) and arrive at the same time each day. Vehicle examinations carried out at Barton Hill are: No 1, every seven days; No 4 every 28 days and No 7, three-monthly. Van interiors are cleaned daily, and exteriors at weekends. Two sets of passenger coaches are maintained: one for South Wales & West — mostly working to Weymouth; the other being a Waterman set working Rhymney–Cardiff.

Above:
'Hawthorn' class 2-4-0 broad gauge *Avonside*, originally named *Slaughter*, built by Slaughter, Gruning & Co, Bristol. *LPC*

Left:
Inside Peckett's Atlas Works: in the foreground are partly completed saddle tanks to fit over boilers in the background. *Author's collection*

Above:
'74xx' class 0-6-0PT No 7436 in St Philip's Marsh shed, 6 February 1964.
Revd Alan Newman

Right:
Class 45 No 75 and Class 47 No 1599 at Bath Road shed, 23 April 1969.
Revd Alan Newman

Right:
Fall pipe with 'GWR — Wolverhampton — Nov 1871' cast on, at the rear of No 3 depot, Barton Hill, 22 January 1996. *Author*

Below:
Barton Hill fuel bay, an additional siding is being laid on 22 January 1996. No 47761 stands on the right. *Author*

Opposite above:
Barton Hill: a van being updated, 22 January 1996. *Author*

Opposite below:
The Res depot, Barton Hill: on 22 January 1996 Nos 08897 and 37412 stand to the right of the building formerly of Dutch barn construction without cladding. *Author*

94032
NLA

STOP
STOP

From 23 July 1995 the works also became Barton Hill diesel depot (code BK), the 1872 GWR wagon repair shop building being utilised. One of the two roads has an inspection pit and the other an ordinary flush floor. As the former wagon shop pit was too shallow for locomotive purposes and a side pit was required for such work as changing brake blocks, it was found that raising the track was a cheaper solution than enlarging the pit. The depot can carry out 'A' (weekly) examinations to about 10 Class 47 and one Class 08 each 24hr. Major repairs are sent to Crewe. To guard against runaways, or engines entering without the men inside being aware, for safety both sheds are protected by derailers. When a derailer is placed down enabling a vehicle to pass, blue lights flash and a Klaxon horn sounds a warning. The only locomotives permanently allocated to the shed are three Class 08 shunters which bear a unicorn emblem — part of the City of Bristol coat of arms — and will carry names of the Bristol Channel islands: Steep Holm, Flat Holm and Lundy. The former blacksmiths' shop is now the base of 60 Bristol Res drivers. This amenities block has a locker room, shower room, smoking room and toilets.

Each item removed from the stores is entered on the IMACS Depot Terminal System and when the number of a particular item declines to a predetermined level, the computer orders more. Peculiarly, railway items come from Doncaster, the remainder are ordered from approved private suppliers. Some items have a limited shelf life and to avoid deterioration, older stock of such things as brake hoses is brought to the front to be used first. Some of the Kingsland Road sidings have been retained and used for storing vehicles proceeding to or from Barton Hill. The rest have been lifted and the area used by Signalling and Telecommunications.

Locomotive building was an important Bristol industry — in fact more engines were built at Bristol than at Derby, Darlington or Doncaster. Bristol built 24.8% of British broad gauge engines and from 1864 to 1881, one in nine of the locomotives built in Britain was made at Bristol. In 1837 Henry Stothert, a Bath engineer who expanded to Bristol, founded the Avonside Ironworks at St Philip's; Edward Slaughter, an assistant engineer to Brunel, joined the company in 1841. Locomotive construction began in 1840 and engines were supplied to most major

railway companies, a high proportion going to broad gauge lines such as the GWR, B&E and Bristol & Gloucester. A new partnership, Slaughter, Gruning & Co formed in 1856, was dissolved in 1864 when the firm was registered as the Avonside Engine Co Ltd — only the second locomotive firm to become a public limited company under the terms of the 1862 Companies Act. In 1865 Avonside built a GWR 'Hawthorn' class 2-4-0 and named it *Slaughter*, but, so the story goes, one of the Great Western directors strolling up to look at the engine hauling his train was horrified to see its name, had it removed and *Avonside* substituted. In 1871 the first of a hundred or so Fairlie Patent locomotives left Avonside works and additionally about 30 single-ended types were built. In the mid-1870s Avonside was employing a workforce of 800–900 and building about 50 locomotives annually, well over half of them for export to India, South America and Australasia, but by the end of that decade the world market for main line locomotives had become highly competitive and this, together with a worldwide trade recession, forced the Bristol firm into a final voluntary liquidation in 1881 after a brief period of recapitalisation following a collapse of two years before.

Fox, Walker & Co established the Atlas Locomotive Works in Deep Pit Road, St George, the same year that the Avonside Engine Co was formed. Access to the Atlas factory was by way of a colliery branch line from Kingswood Junction. The firm specialised in four- and six-wheeled industrial saddle tank engines in addition to locomotives for the new narrow gauge systems being laid in many countries. The largest Fox, Walker engines were nine 0-6-0STs built in 1874/5 for the Somerset & Dorset Railway.

Left:
Van doors and wheel sets at Barton Hill, 22 January 1996. No 47761 stands beyond the 12.5-tonne crane. *Author*

Above:
Barton Hill: raised track outside No 3 depot, 22 January 1996. An oil interceptor is on the left. *Author*

Some 400 locomotives were built before the firm failed in December 1878 as a result of costly and unsuccessful experimental work with street tramway engines and a complex patent machine — Handyside's Step Gradient Locomotive. Edwin Walker, having salvaged patterns and spares from the firm, leased a part of the old Avonside Ironworks and in 1882 started to trade as the Avonside Engine Co. He continued the Fox, Walker policy of building industrial tank engines and narrow gauge locomotives for export. In 1904 a new partnership was formed and a modern factory erected adjacent to Fishponds station, locomotive building commencing there in 1905. The firm became a limited company in 1909, this time a private one, and survived until the slump of the 1930s brought voluntary liquidation. The works closed in 1935, the goodwill being taken over by the Hunslet Engine Co Ltd and the factory building being bought by Parnall & Co Ltd. Meanwhile the Atlas Locomotive Works had been taken over by Thomas Peckett who formed a partnership, Thomas Peckett & Sons, in 1880. His building policy was similar to Walker's in that industrial locomotives, substantially to Walker's design, were built. Peckett's, however, never established themselves in the narrow gauge export market. The firm became a private limited company in 1914, but in the late 1940s failed to change over to building diesels which most industrial users then required. The last locomotive left the works in February 1961 when the firm was taken over by the Reed Crane & Hoist Co Ltd. A total of 2,166 engines had been built since 1864: an annual average output of just over 22.

The Bristol Industrial Museum has preserved 0-6-0STs by each of the three builders.

PASSENGER STATIONS AND GOODS SHEDS

Brunel's imposing Tudor-style Bristol terminus which matched many of the bridges and tunnels from Bath westwards, was built on fields called Temple Meads. Constructed on brick arches 15ft above ground level, it formed a parallelogram 408ft by 114ft. On the north — the old departure side — on the ground floor were the booking offices. Luggage was carried up in lifts, but passengers used stairs to reach the platforms. The walls were in Bath stone, while the impressive timber cantilever train shed roof had a span of 72ft unsupported by any crosstie or abutment, being carried on octagonal iron piers with four centred arches. Each principal was formed of two frameworks like cranes, meeting in the centre of the roof, the weight being carried on the octagonal columns and the tail ends of the frames held down by the side walls. As the two frames did not press against each other where they met, there was no outward thrust. The octagonal piers were rather close to the edge of the platforms and caused an awkward obstruction to passengers, but the difficulty was obviated when the broad gauge was abolished and the platforms could be widened. The glazed roof had a length of 220ft. Beyond the train shed — very much like the nave of a church, the platforms being the aisles — was the flat-ceilinged chancel where locomotives were stored. Forsaking the Gothic, the ceiling was supported by closely spaced, slender unembellished iron columns. Above and in front of this engine shed, was the four-storey office block and it was not unknown for steam from engines to seep up through the floorboards.

The symmetrical Tudor façade facing Temple Gate has angle turrets and a centre oriel above which are the arms of the cities of Bristol and London adopted by the GWR for its own arms. Originally there were two flanking gateways, the departure side on the left having a clock, but the right-hand gateway was removed, probably when the tram terminus along the southern wall of the train shed was electrified. The whole impression of the original station was that of a gentleman's country seat and would have boosted the confidence of nervous early travellers.

Below:
The Temple Gate frontage of Brunel's terminus, 29 May 1980. *Author*

When the B&E opened in 1841 it used the GWR terminus at Bristol. This involved backing trains into or out of the station, and so, in 1845, it opened its own terminus at right angles to the east end of the GWR station. It was a simple wooden construction with overall roof lacking the height of its nearby GWR counterpart. It spanned two platform roads and two centre roads for stabling coaches. Because of its construction and position near the cattle market, it was popularly known as the 'cow shed'. A double track curve linked the two railways and an 'express platform' was provided by the B&E on the Up line, but was used by both Up and Down expresses. This platform was not invariably used for such trains, as in 1862 the Down 'Flying Dutchman' ran to the end of the curve and then backed into the B&E terminus. In 1852 the B&E went one better than the GWR for it opened a refreshment room at its station. The same year, work started on the new office block to the south of the station approach. Completed in October 1854, it was designed by F. C. Fripp whose initials are carried high on the north side of the building which is of symmetrical Jacobean design with shaped gables and twin towers with ogee caps. When the

Above:
Sir Robert Baden-Powell leaving Temple Meads by the rarely photographed southeast exit on his way to the Jamboree *c*1920. *M. J. Tozer collection*

Left:
Water bowsers at Temple Meads standing ready for use, 21 August 1995. *Author*

Right:
Oven in Brunel's terminus, 4 September 1986. *Author*

B&E became amalgamated with the GWR in 1876, the offices were taken over by the GWR's Bristol Traffic Division.

In 1861 a plan backed by the GWR was put forward for extending the B&E, MR and GWR to a new central station in Queen Square, but this suggestion was rejected by a narrow majority of the city council, so the three companies fell back on the idea of building a new joint station at Temple Meads. It was certainly necessary; in 1863 only two platforms had to deal with GWR trains running to London, Westbury and New Passage Pier, and MR services to Birmingham.

In 1865 the three companies obtained an Act to build a new joint station, but because of disputes regarding the proportionate division of the cost, another six years passed before work was even begun and a further six were needed for the task to be completed. Meanwhile in 1871 a new thoroughfare, Victoria Street/Temple Street, later served by trams, was made to link the city with the joint station. The B&E terminus was demolished and a great curved train shed with a span of 125ft built on the site of the former B&E express platform to cover the new platforms. Vernon & Evans of the Central Iron Works, Cheltenham, were contractors for metal work. Brunel's original train shed was lengthened in similar style to the original, though the roof supports were metal, not wood and had thin ties. The enlarged station, V-shaped in plan, opened on 1 January 1878, had a fine rising approach road to an architecturally pleasing main entrance with offices and a 100ft-high clock tower of Draycott stone approximately on the site of the old B&E terminus. Sir Matthew Digby Wyatt, an old friend of Brunel who has assisted him with his 1854 Paddington station, was architect for the extension and his design blended with the original. Francis Fox of the B&E took his share in the scheme, the green and gold exterior canopy almost certainly being of his design because it is virtually identical to the one he designed for Weston-super-Mare. Each company had its own booking office within the Great Hall and passengers for the respective companies entered by separate doors, a scroll above each bearing the appropriate legend — the MR the left-hand door, the B&E centre, and the GWR the right. Inside the entrance doors can still be seen the pinewood porters' booths, but the imposing pine entrance doors were removed as they had to be left open and this caused the entrance hall to be cold and draughty in winter so today they have been replaced by automatic doors. The first section of the new station opened on 6 July 1874. Access to the Down platforms was by a road leading south of the B&E offices and passing under the line. The red brick walls of the interior of the curved train shed have been cleaned since the abolition of steam, allowing the effective black brick decoration at the top to be seen for the first time in many years.

The extended station had seven platforms and in the new train shed, counting from the east, were Nos 1 to 4. No 1, the Down Main, was 286yd long and Nos 2–4 were each of 143yd length, the island platform being used mainly for down MR trains to facilitate interchange as passengers could walk straight across the platform to a Down GWR train. Platform No 4 was the GWR Up Main; platforms No 5 and 6 were the lengthened southern platform of the original terminus, the outer end of which was used for MR departures and the inner for New Passage or, later, South Wales trains. Platform No 7 was for arriving and departing Clifton Down and Avonmouth trains. Refreshment rooms were built in the apex between the old and new stations.

Even before its completion the station was inadequate, several minor accidents between 1871 and 1876 being attributed by Board of Trade inspectors directly, or indirectly, to the congested state of the new station. The bridge over the New Cut was widened so that the Down platform could be lengthened and a Down bay brought into use in October 1892, the narrowing of the gauge allowing an additional island platform six years later. In 1902 a wooden footbridge was built in the terminal station spoiling the vista of Brunel's roof; it was eventually removed in the 1930s.

A report on 11 August 1906 revealed the station's shortcomings. Although Platform No 1 was 963ft in length, ramp to ramp, only 574ft was available without blocking the entrance to Platform No 2 and the engine shed road. MR trains used No 2 and, especially during summer, they overlapped the platform at the east end by three to four coaches so in order to exchange vehicles with the GWR, the train had to be drawn forward and then fouled No 1 line. Frequently a string of engines occupied platform No 3 and stood there until they could be disposed of. At times the station was so congested the trains stood block to block from Bath to Bristol on one side and Yatton to Bristol on the other. In 1914 the GWR decided to remodel the permanent way, extend the station and install modern labour-saving signalling, but the outbreak of World War 1 prevented these plans from going ahead.

Below:
No 47820 arrives at Bristol Parkway on 28 August 1990 with the 'Devon Scot', 07.10 Plymouth–Aberdeen. *Author*

Right:
2-6-0 No 6319 of St Philip's Marsh shed, calls at Redland with a Temple Meads–Severn Beach train, 19 April 1960.
E. T. Gill/Revd Brian Arman collection

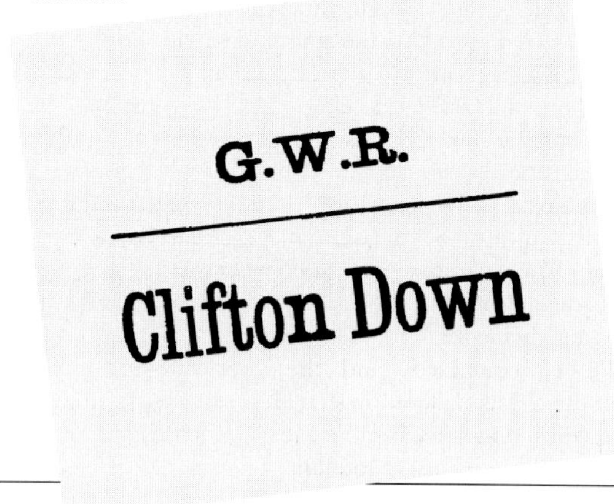

By the 1920s traffic had grown to such an extent that on Bank Holidays trains were held in block from Highbridge waiting for a platform at Bristol and often had to stand outside Temple Meads for an hour. On summer Saturdays between 1920 and 1930 it was not unknown for local trains from Bath and Radstock to take two hours or more for the last mile into the station and on at least one occasion, the time for the last mile was 3hr 20min. The railway could not be blamed for this state of affairs as the only room for extension was over Bristol Corporation's cattle market and to this the city council raised objections. The only immediate post-World War 1 improvement was doubling the width of the footbridge spanning the platforms of the through station and providing a new exit from it direct to the approach road. This work was completed on 10 July 1920. Then in 1929, as a measure to assist in easing the depression, the government made loans to carry out large public works and it was agreed that the enlargement of Temple Meads would qualify. Under the direction of P. E. Culverhouse the station was enlarged to more than twice its size, the number of platforms being increased from 9 to 15, a large slice of the adjoining market being bought. The longest platform, Nos 9 and 10 combined, and the 10th longest in the country, was 1,366ft in length compared with the previous longest at Temple Meads of 920ft, the length of all the platforms totalling two miles. All main platforms were provided with refreshment and waiting rooms. Work began in November 1930, Shanks & McEwan of Glasgow being the main contractors. The roofs of the new platforms were of the 'umbrella' or 'arcade' type, while the buildings were constructed of white or brown Carrara glazed bricks on a grey concrete plinth. During the conversion of the old through station, when the two island platforms of the 1878 station were taken out to allow the old main Up and Down through platforms to be widened, both Up and Down traffic operated from the new platforms Nos 1 to 5 built on the site of the Down approach road. The reconstructed old through platforms were opened on 25 March 1935, the job having taken more than two years. The completed station had five Up and five Down platforms, a bay for Portishead trains and four platforms in the old terminus. The enlarged Temple Meads was completed in December 1935 and became a 'closed' station. The booking office, given a modern cast iron and bronze front, was set back to give a spacious circulating area. Passengers gained their platform by a 300ft-long and 30ft-wide subway also giving access to hairdressing saloons, toilets and baths, while parcels were carried in electric trolleys along a special subway connecting the parcels depot with all platforms. Electric lifts linked platforms with the subway. In three places scissors crossings were provided between the platform and adjacent through roads so that two trains could be accommodated simultaneously along one platform face. Rather surprisingly, gas lighting was used for the new platforms and remained in use until 1960 when replaced by fluorescent tubes. This lighting in turn was superseded by high pressure sodium giving much brighter illumination and causing the number of cars stolen from the approach road to decrease by 50%. At the same time the tower was floodlit.

On 25 June 1940 Bristol had its first air raid, the prime target being Temple Meads since it was a key traffic centre. It received little damage, but on 2 December the station was hit and various suburban lines put out of action for several hours. On 6 December there were heavy casualties on the 7.10pm to Salisbury which received a direct hit at the station; the same day a bomb struck No 2 Tunnel at St Anne's Park. On 3 January 1941 the station was the target for incendiary bombs and when all were thought to have been extinguished, one lodged behind the clock started a fire which destroyed the tower's spire and burnt out the telegraph office and telephone exchange above the booking office, the latter being damaged by water. Passengers were soon buying tickets at army huts hurriedly erected in the station approach.

Bristolians were afraid that light from the fireboxes of the many locomotives in their city might be seen by enemy raiders, so one night

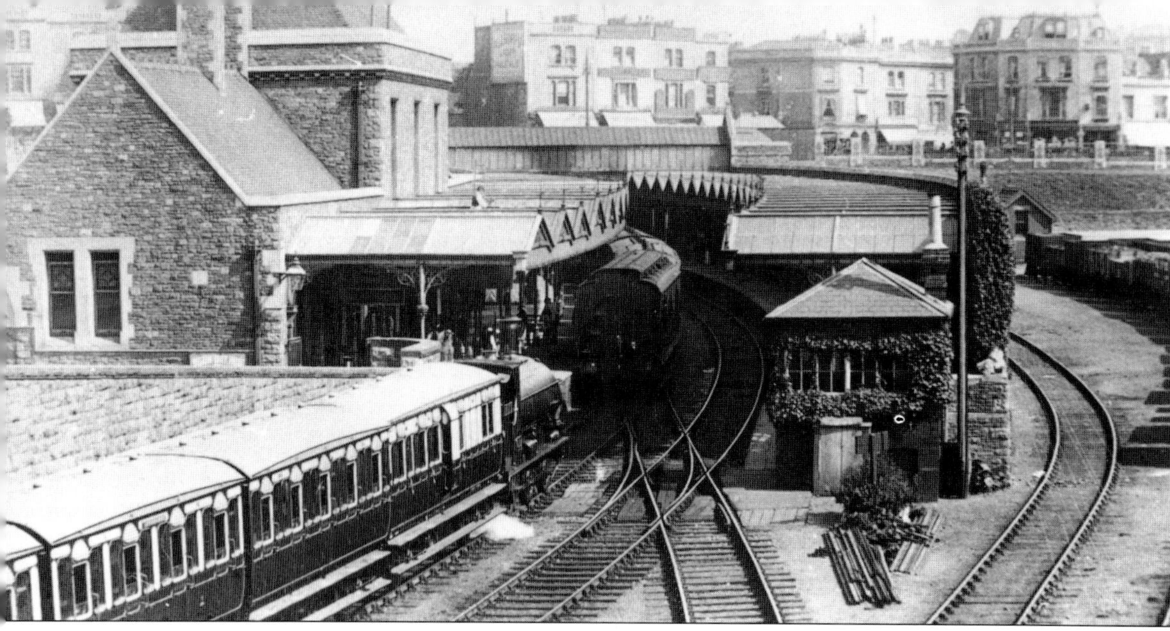

Above:
An 0-6-0ST heads an Up train at Clifton Down station *c*1905. It is very close to the train in front. To the right of the ivy-covered signalbox is the extensive coal yard. *M. J. Tozer collection*

Left:
'Steam Tavern', a feature of which is the inverted signs. It is the former station building at Clifton Down and its architecture indicates its original importance in this select suburb of Bristol, 9 October 1995. *Author*

Above right:
The BPRP's terminal station at Hotwells, nestling almost below Clifton Suspension Bridge, *c*1910. *M. J. Tozer collection*

Right:
No 153353 at Shirehampton on 9 October 1995 working the 11.48 Severn Beach–Temple Meads. *Author*

the RAF flew over Bristol to determine the danger. It reported: 'Intense observation from the air did not reveal any lighting due to railway operations.' In fact only very large lights were visible to aircraft and fireboxes did not enter this category.

Bristol was an important centre for both goods traffic and military personnel, wartime traffic often being hectic. Tunnels below Temple Meads were used as an air raid shelter for passengers and staff, and also as an emergency centre for key railwaymen. In both world wars wounded servicemen were unloaded at Platform No 14 and taken direct to ambulances which carried them to hospitals in and around Bristol. In anticipation of communications to and from the Divisional Office being severed, a camp coach fitted with radio equipment was stabled at Severn Beach and, had a breakdown in communications occurred at Temple Meads, would have been taken to Bristol. During World War 2 a five-coach set of Super Saloons was kept at Dr Day's Sidings and if a VIP arrived at Bristol airport he was taken by road to Temple Meads where he boarded the special, drawn by the 'Castle' class engine acting as passenger station pilot, nonstop to Paddington. After arrival, the engine and coaches promptly returned to Bristol. Following the cessation of hostilities, because the war had interfered with normal 'learn by experience' training of signal linesmen, from November 1946 the vault below Platform No 9 was used as a technical school for a three months' intensive course in the installation and upkeep of mechanical and electrical signalling apparatus, points, track circuits and telephones.

With the contraction of passenger traffic in the 1960s, the platforms in Brunel's train shed, ironically known as the 'Midland station' because it was used by LMS/LMR trains, became redundant; it was closed on 12 September 1965 and became a car park the following year. This part of Temple Meads is one of the oldest surviving main line terminal stations remaining in an almost unaltered state and is a Grade 1 listed building. Refurbishment in 1991 involved painting and highlighting details in the Wyatt train shed with different colours and the retiling of the subway to give it a more modern appearance. The Brunel Engineering Centre Trust has taken the lease of the original terminal buildings and sub-leases part to the Exploratory — a children's 'hands-on' science exhibition. Staff working at Temple Meads in December 1995 numbered 55 plus 31 in the travel

centre and 61, many part-time, in the travel enquiry bureau.

Bristol Parkway station opened on 1 May 1972 and has played its part in the continuing vitality of rail passenger travel in the Bristol area. Messrs Stone & Co won the contract for £50,000 of building a basic new station, car park and approach roads at Stoke Gifford on the site of the redundant marshalling yard. It has become a great success as more than 1,000 passengers use it daily, the station proving particularly convenient to motorists living on the north side of Bristol, while drivers from the Bath area wishing to travel north can drive to the station, park and catch a train from there; a rather speedier way than changing at Temple Meads. As Parkway proved such a success, its facilities were improved two years later when platform canopies and a full covering to the footbridge were provided. In December 1995 there were eight staff plus four in the travel centre.

The platform side of the wall of Redland station is painted with very large flowers to deter graffiti artists. Immediately to the west is a three-span cast iron footbridge, Grade 2 listed, which carries Lovers' Walk across the line. Clifton Down station was most imposing in its heyday. In modified Gothic style, it had a superb mansion-like booking hall with a huge fireplace at either end. The platforms were formerly sheltered by a ridge and furrow roof with fluted glass. The station building is now the 'Steam Tavern', a feature of which is that all signs and advertisements are inverted. Clifton Down still retains a crossing loop as it is the only passing station on the single line between Stapleton Road and Avonmouth Dock. Flats have been built on the site of the once-important coal yard.

Hotwells, the terminus of the Bristol Port Railway, was situated in a cramped position in the Avon Gorge almost immediately below Clifton Suspension Bridge. The three roads were connected

Above left:
No W55032 at Severn Beach with the 10.08 to Temple Meads, 25 July 1974. *Author*

Left:
Diesel railcars No W23 and W25 leave Clifton Bridge for Portishead on 13 November 1958. The 1907 signalbox can be seen at the far end of the Up platform. *E. T. Gill/Revd Brian Arman collection*

Top:
'57xx' class 0-6-0PT No 3748 viewed at Henbury with the 4.16pm Lawrence Hill–Avonmouth on 25 May 1960. *E. T. Gill/Revd Brian Arman collection*

Above:
Railmotor with 'Bath' on the headboard, calls at Ashton Gate *c*1908 with a train from Portishead. An 0-6-0ST stands on the line leading to Ashton Meadows sidings. *Author's collection*

by a turntable. In its latter days, to obtain maximum use of the 280ft-long platform, the engine stopped just short of the crossover which replaced the turntable, uncoupled and moved over to the parallel road where a wire hawser with a hook at each end was linked between the drawbar of the engine and the leading coach axle. The driver then drew forward gently pulling the train of about six four-wheeled coaches into the station, the guard applying the brake as his van approached the platform. The two-storey stone building was at the terminal end of the platform, trains being on a level with the upper storey and until 1893 the station had a refreshment room. Hotwells closed on 19 September 1921 when the line was cut back to Hotwells Extension Platform which had opened on 14 May 1917 as a wartime expedient so that workmen's trains of eight bogies could be handled. The Extension Platform was closed on 3 July 1922 as the site of the BPRP line to Sneyd Park Junction was required for a new road (Portway) to Avonmouth.

Ashton Gate Platform on the Portishead branch has had an interesting history. A simple wooden structure, it opened solely for football traffic on 15 September 1906, closed on 1 November 1917 and reopened on 23 May 1926. Close to Bristol City football ground, at times it received through specials from the SR drawn by Pacifics and when football traffic was heavy, permission was given for an Up train to be started from the Down platform under supervision of an inspector and with a groundsman at the crossover points to clip them for the passage of the train. Closed on 7 September 1964, it was reopened for football specials, the first train to use it after reopening being a special three-car DMU from Birmingham on 29 September 1970. Since 1977 control problems have led to its disuse, Parson Street being used instead. Any such specials today use Temple Meads. Ashton Gate Platform enjoyed a new lease of life when it was reopened temporarily to deal with people travelling to and from Dr Billy Graham's 'Mission England' held at the football stadium from 12–19 May 1984.

Because Temple Meads was unable to cope with any more trains, St Philip's station was opened on 2 May 1870, a timber-built terminal station of one platform covered by a ridge and furrow glass roof. In the rationalisation following the enlargement of Temple Meads in the 1930s, it closed on 21 September 1953.

The original Yate station, designed either by Brunel himself or a member of his staff, closed to passengers on 4 January 1965 and to goods on 20 June 1966. Since then Yate has developed as a new town and commuter traffic into Bristol has increased enormously. A new station with staggered platforms was officially opened at Yate on 11 May 1989 and to the public four days later. Funded by Avon County Council, it cost £140,000. The feeder bus service from Chipping Sodbury and North Yate which met most arrivals and departures was extended to Hawkesbury Upton and Horton in June 1990.

On 25 October 1995 as the largest office block in Western Europe, the Ministry of Defence complex at Filton Abbey Wood, was nearing completion, work started on building a new station to serve it. Filton Abbey Wood is about 1/4 mile south of Filton station. Filton Abbey Wood station is a joint venture between the former county council, South Wales & West Railway, Railtrack, the Ministry of Defence and BR Property Board and cost £1.4 million. Opened to the public on 11 March 1996 the first train was the 05.45 Gloucester–Plymouth. The station is served by 62 trains Mondays–Fridays with direct peak hour services from Westbury, Bath, Weston-super-Mare, Cardiff and Gloucester. The enhanced service on the Westbury-Bath–Filton Abbey Wood route is underwritten by the new South Gloucestershire Council under a revenue guarantee/profit share agreement. The station is served by special 1/4-hourly Rail Link buses run from Colston Avenue to the University of the West of England via Abbey Wood station and the offices of Bristol & West, Sun Life and Hewlett Packard. The station is within easy walking distance of the Ministry of Defence offices. When purchasing a rail ticket to Abbey Wood it can be made valid for the Rail Link service by paying an additional low fare. On 19 March 1996 the station was officially opened jointly by the Minister of Public Transport, Steven Norris MP, and the Chair of Avon County Council, Councillor Rosalie Walker.

Temple Meads goods yard was situated at right angles to the passenger terminus and 12ft below, access being by turntables and two hydraulically powered lifts acting rather like a pair of scales, each lowering one wagon and at the same time raising another, the operation taking about half a minute. The goods shed, 326ft by 138ft, was equipped with cranes for loading and unloading wagons, the depot holding 209. The shed was an example of Brunel's functional design at its best. It had a central span of 60ft plus two side spans of 40ft each. Columns were placed at 35ft centres along the building, and longitudinal trusses were provided in addition to the transverse trusses. Both sets used timber members in compression with wrought iron ties. The combination of solid looking timbers and light metal ties created a roof both functional and elegant. Hydraulic capstans and horses were used for making wagon movements within the shed, Brunel remarking, 'We have several

Above left:
An Up DMU from Portishead to Temple Meads approaches Clifton Bridge station on 30 April 1959. Six coaches are stabled in the siding on the left. A tug is setting off downstream. The cradle slung below the centre of the suspension bridge is used by painters and can be moved as work progresses.
E. T. Gill/Revd Brian Arman collection

Right:
The arrival of No 150247, the first train at the new Yate station, the 06.52 Gloucester–Temple Meads, on 15 May 1989. *Author*

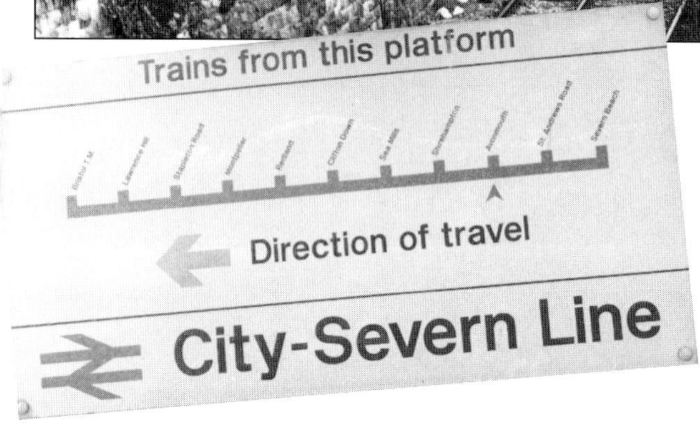

small capstan heads in different parts of the station, which are always in motion running round and a porter takes a turn round one of these with a rope which is hooked on to any carriage which he wishes to move.' In 1844 the GWR had six trains using the shed. An Up GWR goods arrived at 7.30pm and the Bristol & Gloucester goods had to leave before it arrived, which meant that the BGR closed its acceptance at 5pm; even then, 2½hr was insufficient time to complete loading and invoicing. Competitive road transport accepted goods until 4pm and arrived in Gloucester for next morning's delivery so the railway had but little advantage, yet its host, the GWR, did not close until 8pm and more goods were received between 5pm and 8pm than during the rest of the day. The shed handled B&E traffic until 1 May 1850 when the latter opened its own shed at Pylle Hill. The GWR depot was also used by the MR when that company took over the Bristol & Gloucester, standard gauge rails having to be laid in 1854. The depot was inadequate to deal with the requirements of expanding traffic, so between 1874 and 1876 it was remodelled. Rowland Brotherhood of Chippenham obtained the contract. To give extra space, the old dock he had constructed about 35 years — before to give barges access to the Floating Harbour — was filled in and replaced by a new barge wharf with steam and hydraulic cranes. The whole surface of the goods yard was then raised 3ft 6in and the layout rearranged, the new shed having six platforms averaging 445ft in length and

Top:
Clifton Down station on 9 October 1995, view Up. The buildings on the right are on the site of the former coal yard. Double track is retained as a passing loop. *Author*

Above left:
Train indicator at Avonmouth, 9 October 1995. *Author*

Above right:
Temple Meads goods yard with shed beyond *c*1920. The wall of the passenger station can be seen on the far left. *Author's collection*

Below right:
Temple Meads goods depot in the 1930s. Notice the very narrow Temple Meads Goods signalbox and, centre, grounded coach body. *Author's collection*

accommodation for 200 wagons, with space for a further 232 in the open yard. As delays caused by using the lifts were unacceptable, an incline was built to the lower level so that a locomotive could shunt trucks to and from the depot; this 1 in 60 gradient assisted shunting as it made a natural hump yard. As the volume of traffic flowing into Bristol was much smaller than outwards, No 1 platform was used for unloading and the other five for loading, except for No 2 which was used until 9am for unloading inwards London goods. Wagons received on the two inwards berths could be shunted round when empty to the outwards loading roads by capstan and horse power without interfering with either the unloading operations or the shunting work at the other end of the yard. In 1908 over 450 wagons had to be dispatched from the depot within six or seven hours. That year the depot had a clerical staff of almost 1,000 to deal with all the invoicing, correspondence and accounts concerning goods traffic in the Bristol area.

All goods trains and engines to and from the main lines had to work over a short section of single line; at times this certainly militated against punctual working. By 1914 1,600–1,700 wagons went in and out of the depot daily, this figure including those for Redcliff Sidings. These sidings were an offshoot of Temple Meads and were where mineral, flour and grain traffic was accommodated, Temple Meads itself being confined to general goods except for consignments of galvanised iron which were loaded at the waterside. Nineteen trains conveying 600 wagons were dispatched from Temple Meads between 6pm and 6am.

Right:
Plans of Temple Meads goods station 1845 and 1935.

Opposite above:
Shunting capstan and wagon traverser at the LMS St Philip's goods depot, 1938.
Author's collection

Opposite centre:
Canon's Marsh goods depot *c*1910. Chalked on the column is: 'H'bridge, Burnham, Stoke Canon, Hele, Bradninch, Cullompton, Y'verton, Hemyock, Ilfracombe, Wells'. A box of Victoria chicken meal is in the lower right-hand corner.
Author's collection

Opposite below:
Programme of annual outing of LMS St Philip's goods dept clerical and supervisory staff, Bristol to Scotland, May 1929.

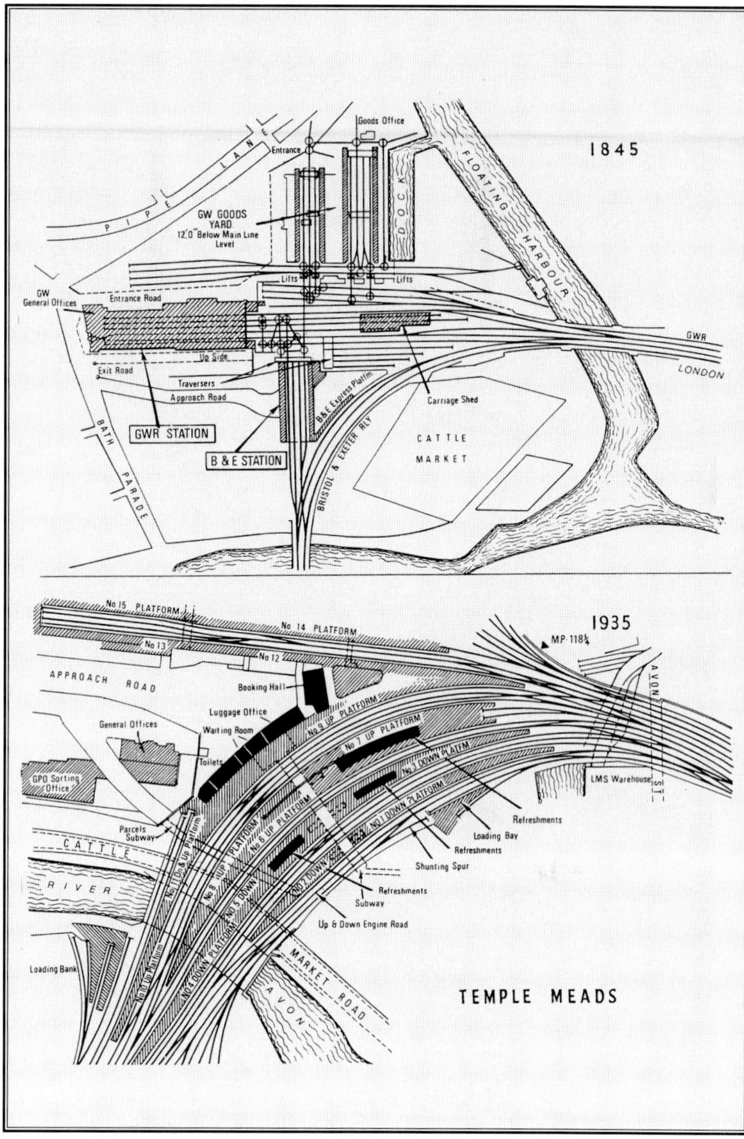

The five outwards platforms in the 1876 Temple Meads goods depot were divided into 16 loading berths according to districts and trains. This unique practice required all carmen, employed either by the GWR or by private firms, when bringing in goods to deliver them to a particular berth, thus reducing porterage and trucking to a minimum. The carmen usually loaded their lorries in the city in such a manner as to facilitate unloading at the different berths. It was rare for goods to be dropped off at the wrong berth because each checker had a good knowledge of stations serviced by his berth. At platforms where there were two loading lines, access to the wagons on the second line was by placing a loading board across from the inner to the outer wagon. In 1914 competition at Bristol for parcels traffic was so great that the GWR paid a tonnage bonus to parcel van men and they tried hard to capture traffic consigned to the MR route. In the 1920s, between 3pm and 5pm, approximately 200 loads (2,000 consignments) were carted into the depot. Wagons arriving were placed on the line serving the long No 1 platform and, after being unloaded, were worked by gravitation and capstan shunters to the bottleneck road at the Victoria Street end of the yard from where they were worked by capstans into the long storage siding, or into the outwards loading lines. At this date, as outwards

Continued on page 115

GOODS DEPARTMENT CLERICAL AND SUPERVISORY STAFF.

BRISTOL (ST. PHILIPS) STATION

Annual Outing

EDINBURGH FORTH BRIDGE and STIRLING

MAY 10th, 11th & 12th, 1929

M.................

Your Bedroom No. 134

GEO. W. DION, *Hon. Secretary.*
J. E. PRIDMORE, *Hon. Treasurer.*

Friday, 10th May

Depart Temple Meads ... ... 12 20 p.m.

Lunch on Train.
Tomato Soup
Cold Salmon. Mayonnaise Sauce
Roast Beef.
Green Vegetables. Potatoes.
Pear Conde.
Cheese. Salad.

Tea on train (if desired), charge 1s. per head 5 0 p.m.

[D]inner on Train ... ... 7 0 p.m.

Mock Turtle.
Boiled Turbot. Anchovy Sauce.
Chicken Paysanne.
Roast Lamb.
Green Vegetables and Potatoes.
Macedoine of Fruit.
Cheese. Salad.

[P]rinces St., Edinburgh ... ... 10 0 p.m.

[G]eorge Hotel, George Street, for the night : [a]t 5 minutes' walk from Station.

Saturday, 11th May

Breakfast ... ... 8 0 a.m.

Tea or Coffee.
Porridge, Grape Nuts or Stewed Prunes and Figs.
Fried Whiting or Loch Fyne Kippers.
Grilled Wiltshire Bacon and Sausage.
Tomatoes or Liver and Bacon.
Eggs, Fried, Boiled or Poached.

Depart Princes Street Station, Platform No. 1 for Stirling ... ... 9 25 a.m.

Arriving at ... ... 10 19 a.m.

Arrangements have been made for those desiring to visit the Castle.

Leave Stirling at ... ... 1 0 p.m.

Lunch served immediately on leaving.
Creme Portugaise.
Fried Fillet Sole. Lemon.
Roast Mutton. Red Currant Jelly.
Green Vegetables. New Potatoes.
Compote of Fruit and Custard.
Cheese and Watercress.

Arrive Edinburgh ... ... 2 15 p.m.

Motors will meet the party and will proceed via Princes Street, Holyrood Palace, John Knox's House, St. Giles Cathedral to the Castle (about 30 minutes will be allowed to inspect the Castle and Scottish War Memorial); after leaving Castle, motors will proceed via Haymarket, Zoo Gardens, &c., to Dalmeny Station, L. & N. E., departing at 4.0 p.m. over the Forth Bridge and alighting at North Queensferry.

Returning from North Queensferry Pier at 4.30 p.m. by Ferry Boat to South Queensferry.

Motors will then proceed back to Edinburgh for tea at the George Hotel ... ...

The London Midland and Scottish Railway Company's

GOODS STATIONS AND DEPOTS

IN

BRISTOL.

ST. PHILIP'S GOODS STATION.

This Station is in convenient proximity to all the principal manufactories and business houses. It is fully equipped with a commodious goods shed and up to date electric and hydraulic cranes for the handling and quick despatch of general goods traffic.

There is also extensive outside accommodation with sidings including many cranes capable of lifting machinery and other heavy articles up to 20 tons weight.

A Carriage Dock is provided where furniture vans and other wheeled vehicles can readily be loaded or unloaded.

Coke, Coal, and Lime.—Extensive sidings are provided for dealing with this class of traffic.

Cattle and Horse Docks.—Complete accommodation exists, within easy distance from the local cattle market, for dealing promptly with all descriptions of live stock.

AVONSIDE GOODS STATION.

Is conveniently situated near many of the local manufactories, embracing the following industries, viz.:—flour, grain, manures, iron, tar, lead, oils, oilcake, leather, soap, colours, &c.

The premises have an extensive water frontage with a good supply of crane power (electric, steam and hydraulic) for quickly loading or discharging barges with import or export traffic, into or out of railway trucks.

Warehouse Accommodation.—There are two very commodious warehouses at Avonside depôt well adapted for the storage of flour, cheese, sugar and general dry goods.

Avonside Goods Station.—The Company's Dock is covered in, traffic can, therefore, be unloaded from barge to truck fully protected from the weather.

Care should be taken to consign goods "per L M S route."

KING'S WHARF DEPOT.

These waterside premises are situated close to Bathurst Basin on the Bristol Harbour and Redcliffe Hill. There are extensive cellars for the storage of non-inflammable oils, wax and similar commodities. For the convenience of merchants and traders in the vicinity such traffics as grain, flour, sugar, &c., are accepted for conveyance by barge to rail at Avonside Goods Depot in precisely the same manner as at the stations.

CARTING DEPARTMENT.

The Company have their own road vehicles and are prepared to cart rail traffic to and from the stations on reasonable terms where this service is not already provided for in the rate.

BARGING DEPARTMENT.

The Company have an office situated on the Bristol City Docks near Prince's Street Bridge where arrangements may be made for the collection by barge overside or delivery alongside ship. The fleet of barges is capable of dealing with all ordinary requirements of the Bristol Docks traffic, such as large consignments of grain, flour, &c., and provides a most expeditious means of transfer between ship and rail.

MONTPELIER STATION.

This station, on the Clifton Extension Railway, is situated in the north of Bristol, and is most convenient for Montpelier, Bishopston, Horfield, Cotham, and lower parts of Redland.

It is available for bricks, stone and timber; also coal and all other descriptions of traffic not requiring protection.

Accommodation for horses, carriages and other vehicles.

CLIFTON DOWN STATION.

Situated on the Clifton Extension Railway, in the western suburbs of Bristol.

There is accommodation for horses, carriages, wagons and other wheeled vehicles, and generally for same class of traffic as at Montpelier.

PORTISHEAD DOCK.

The Company can deal with traffic either to or from this point for all stations to which they carry from Bristol. All communications should be addressed to E. Crofts, District Goods Manager, 37, Corn Street, Bristol, or Goods Agent, St. Philip's Station, Bristol.

AVONMOUTH DOCKS.

The Company have provided accommodation for the receipt and forwarding of all descriptions of cargo, including live stock. The arriving or departing by vessels at Avonmouth Docks. The Company's rails are connected with the Dock Committee's Lines, which run to every part of the dock premises.

Care should be taken to consign goods "per L M S route."

traffic from the depot was about 50% greater than inwards, these wagons were insufficient to supply the requirements of the outwards side, but the arrangement reduced very considerably the number of empty wagons which had to be brought into the shed by locomotives and placed into position for loading.

Traffic from east of Bristol was made up into through trucks for principal West of England stations to the extent of 30 wagons a day, while traffic in the reverse direction was made up at Canon's Marsh and dispatched in about 45 trucks. When there was insufficient traffic at Temple Meads to make a through or transfer wagon for the West of England, the goods were carted to Canon's Marsh for loading into through wagons from that depot, a similar arrangement applying in the reverse direction.

To meet the demands of trade, at Temple Meads in 1924 the GWR built a new shed and sidings at a cost of £556,450. To give sufficient area, dilapidated property between Victoria Street and Temple Back was bought. Covering an area of more than five acres, the 15 platforms were under one roof. Each pair of platforms, 30ft wide and 575ft in length, was connected to adjoining ones by means of tip-up balance bridges to facilitate trolleying. Unlike the old shed, each road had a platform. The new depot could accommodate 408 wagons under cover and 330 in the yard. Electric power was used extensively — electric points, electric capstans to move wagons and electric runways to expedite the conveyance of documents between office and shed. Goods were carried by electric platform trucks and an electric telpher could convey up to a ton of goods to any part of the shed. A special carriage chute for dealing with cars, furniture vans and other road vehicles before and after rail conveyance was worked by an electric capstan. Electric lifts served the cellarage (390ft by 100ft) and overhead warehouse. The cellarage was important to satisfy the ever increasing demand at the port for the storage of butter, cheese, lard, bacon and other perishables. In 1934 the depot dealt with

Continued on page 120

Above left:
Rebuilding Temple Meads in October 1934, view Down. *Author's collection*

Below left:
Details of LMS goods facilities at Bristol, 1926.

Below:
Res shunter No 08804 with Royal Mail vans at Temple Meads on 21 August 1995. *Author*

Above:
Bristol Temple Meads West signalbox, March 1970. *D. Payne*

Right:
Building the western extension to Temple Meads. On the left and right can be seen lift shaft towers. Three of the wagons towards the centre are Nos 660, 199 and 192. View *c*1934. *Author's collection*

Below:
GWR gas surface box cover set in the platform, Temple Meads, 31 October 1995. *Author*

Opposite:
The imposing entrance to Temple Meads, 23 August 1995. *Author*

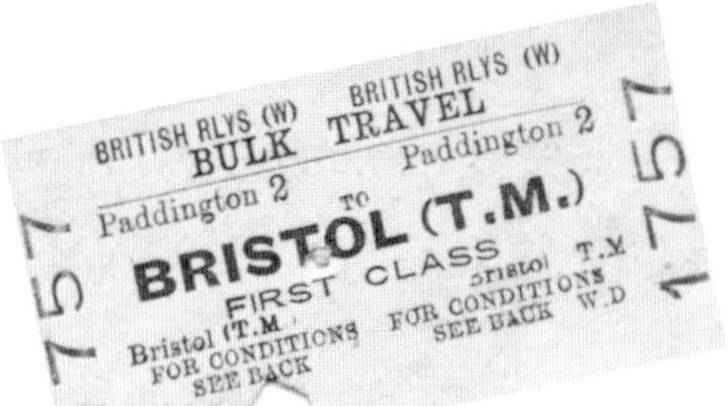

British Rail
No right turn

Above:
From an almost identical viewpoint to the centre photo on page 116 is No 143623 working the 13.18 Temple Meads–Cardiff on 31 October 1995. *Author*

Right:
GWR water surface box cover set in the platform, Temple Meads, 31 October 1995. *Author*

Below right:
'Kerslake Engineer Exeter 1876' cast at the foot of a column supporting Wyatt's train shed, 31 October 1995. *Author*

Opposite above:
General view of Temple Meads from Bath Road bridge, 31 October 1995. *Author*

Opposite, below left:
The ecclesiastical-like interior of the booking hall, 31 October 1995. *Author*

Opposite, below right:
A three-car DMU approaches Avonmouth Dock station on a Severn Beach–Temple Meads working, February 1959.
E. T. Gill/Revd Brian Arman collection

L.M.&S.R. For conditions see back.
THIRD CLASS SINGLE.
L.M.&S.R. For conditions see back
THIRD CLASS SINGLE
1481
Glasgow(Cen.)
Glasgow (Central) To
Glasgow (Cen
AVONMOUTH DOCK
AvonmouthDk
AvonmouthDk
Via Carstairs Crewe
Sev. Tunnel

over 4 million parcels and 1.5 million tons of goods. Latterly a National Carriers Ltd depot, it closed on 1 August 1982 and was demolished shortly afterwards.

The warehouse and goods shed at Canon's Marsh was opened in October 1906. Measuring 540ft by 133ft, it was of ferro-concrete on the Hennebique principle, there being 274 ferro-concrete piles averaging 32ft in depth in the foundations, as the ground, not surprising in view of its name, was soft. 35ft in height, the shed had a floor area of 35,600sq ft. The steel and corrugated iron roof had Rendle's patent glazing. The contractor for the building was Robertson of Bristol. Four roads holding about 97 wagons passed through the building, with a 20ft-wide platform between the two most northerly lines and one of the same dimensions between the southerly line and cartway. The depot was equipped with eight electric cranes and three 30cwt electric hoists. The yard's 22 sidings accommodated 531 wagons. The upper storey of the shed was a warehouse. The depot was important as it gave rail access to the city docks and avoided the extra expense involved in carting or barging and thus relieved pressure on the two oldest depots in the city — Temple Meads and Pylle Hill. Later, increased warehouse accommodation to the extent of over 4,000sq yd was erected at Pylle Hill and new mileage depots were built at St Philip's Marsh and Stapleton Road.

Prior to 1858 the inwards and outwards goods departments of the MR at Bristol were carried on in the GWR's Temple Meads goods depot, but that year, due to an increase in traffic, the MR inwards goods department moved to the MR coal yard at St Philip's where a goods depot was erected. Eight years later it was doubled in size to accommodate the outwards department as well. The building erected by Humphries of Derby measured 180ft by 133ft and was supported on cast iron columns resting on wrought iron girders. Fifteen hydraulic cranes of Sir William Armstrong's patent pattern lifted up to two tons and were so placed that as one raised goods from the trucks to the platform, another lifted goods from the platform to the trucks on the other side. Six traversing tables were worked by hydraulic power and hydraulic capstan engines capable of moving 80 tons drew wagons in or out of the shed. Hydraulic power came from an Armstrong patent accumulator worked by two engines of about 60hp. A feature of the shed adopted from St Pancras passenger station, was that below was spacious cellarage for the storage of over 15,000 hogsheads of Burton and other ales consigned to tradesmen in the area, a new facility which the company had recently developed. The building also stabled 50 horses belonging to the MR, while nearby were the corn lofts. The yard had 20 roads. A carriage dock permitted horse-drawn furniture vans and other wheeled vehicles to be loaded and unloaded, and extensive cattle pens and coal yards adjoined. Access to the goods station and the nearby St Philip's passenger station was by a single line to each. Through the years the shed received improvements such as electric cranes supplementing those of the hydraulic pattern, but with a reduction in goods traffic, the depot which had been renamed Bristol, Midland Road on 15 September 1952, closed on 1 April 1967.

Above:
Entrance to the booking offices from Brunel's train shed, 31 October 1995.
Author

LOCOMOTIVE ALLOCATIONS

BATH ROAD AND ST PHILIP'S MARSH ALLOCATION 1914

0-6-0 'Standard Goods'
238, 504, 674, 792, 886, 1112, 1196, 1205, 1209.

2-4-0T 'Metro'
459, 624, 632, 979, 1456.

0-4-2T '517' class
519, 528, 537, 539, 553, 599, 837, 846.

2-4-0 '806' class
823.

0-6-0ST/PT '850' class
989 PT, 1224 ST, 1916 PT, 1919PT, 1928 PT, 1946 ST, 1952 ST, 1954 PT, 1964 ST, 1978 ST, 1995 PT, 1996 PT, 1998 PT, 2012 PT, 2015 ST, 2017 ST.

0-6-0ST '1076' class
1271, 1589, 1601.

0-6-0ST/PT '1854' class
1712 PT, 1719 PT, 1761 ST, 1794 PT, 1864 PT, 1877 PT, 1889 PT, 1893 ST, 1899 PT.

0-6-0ST '655' class
1746.

0-6-0ST '1813' class
1852.

0-6-0ST/PT '2021' class
2031 ST, 2035 ST, 2044 ST, 2059 ST, 2102 PT, 2115 PT, 2127 ST, 2130 PT, 2158 ST.

2-4-0T '2201' class
2201.

0-6-0 'Dean Goods'
2304, 2308, 2320, 2382, 2383, 2389, 2392, 2395, 2396, 2411, 2415, 2421-23, 2435, 2440, 2461, 2470, 2481, 2485, 2520, 2526, 2533, 2543, 2547, 2551, 2557, 2565, 2580.

0-6-0 '2361' class
2369, 2370, 2376, 2378.

2-6-0 'Aberdare'
2622, 2648.

0-6-0ST/PT '2721' class
2729 ST, 2761 PT, 2776 ST, 2786 ST, 2793 PT.

2-8-0 '2800' class
2809, 2821, 2828, 2854.

4-6-0 'Saint' class
2900 *William Dean*, 2922 *Saint Gabriel*, 2930 *Saint Vincent*, 2946 *Langford Court*, 2971 *Albion*, 2973 *Robins Bolitho*, 2974 *Lord Barrymore*, 2976 *Winterstoke*, 2982 *Lalla Rookh*, 2983 *Red Gauntlet*, 2985 *Peveril of the Peak*, 2986 *Robin Hood*, 2987 *Bride of Lammermoor*, 2990 *Waverley*.

Below:
A Down railmotor hauling trailer No 2, the latter with 'Bristol' above the driver's vestibule, stands at Clifton Bridge c1906. The signalbox on the Up platform was replaced on 25 August 1907 with one at the south end of the same platform. *Author's collection*

2-6-2T '3150' class
3159, 3168.

2-4-0 '3201' class
3201.

2-4-0 '3226' class
3231.

4-4-0 'Duke' class
3254 *Boscawen*, 3268 *River Tamar.*

4-4-0 'Atbara' class
3387 *Roberts*, 4136 *Terrible*, 4144 *Colombo*, 4145 *Dunedin.*

4-4-0 '3521' class
3533.

4-4-0 'City' class
3708 *Killarney*, 3715 *City of Hereford*, 3717 *City of Truro.*

4-4-0 'County' class
3802 *County Clare*, 3807 *County Kilkenny*, 3815 *County of Hants*, 3824 *County of Cornwall*, 3832 *County of Wilts*, 3833 *County of Dorset.*

4-4-0 'Badminton' class
4114 *Shelburne.*

4-4-0 'Flower' class
4153 *Camellia*, 4160 *Carnation*, 4164 *Mignonette*, 4166 *Polyanthus.*

2-6-0 '4300' class
4323, 4324, 4334, 4339.

TOTAL 150

BATH ROAD ALLOCATION 8 JANUARY 1938

0-6-0PT '2021' class
2031.

0-6-0 'Dean Goods'
2485, 2568.

4-6-0 'Saint' class
2913 *Saint Andrew*, 2933 *Bibury Court*, 2934 *Butleigh Court*, 2936 *Cefntilla Court*, 2942 *Fawley Court*, 2943 *Hampton Court*, 2953 *Titley Court*, 2954 *Tockenham Court*, 2955 *Tortworth Court.*

4-4-0 'Bulldog' class
3308, 3330 *Orion*, 3363 *Alfred Baldwin*, 3370 *Sir John Llewelyn*, 3371 *Sir Massey Lopes*, 3376 *River Plym*, 3380 *River Yealm*, 3396 *Natal Colony.*

4-6-0 'Star' class
4019 *Knight Templar*, 4022 *Belgian Monarch*, 4033 *Queen Victoria*, 4035 *Queen Charlotte*, 4041 *Prince of Wales*, 4042 *Prince Albert*, 4043 *Prince Henry*, 4055 *Princess Sophia*, 4057 *Princess Elizabeth*, 4062 *Malmesbury Abbey*, 4069 *Westminster Abbey*, 4071 *Cleeve Abbey.*

4-6-0 'Castle' class
4016 *Knight of the Golden Fleece*, 4081 *Warwick Castle*, 4082 *Windsor Castle*, 4096 *Highclere Castle*, 5025 *Chirk Castle*, 5048 *Earl of Devon*, 5084 *Reading Abbey.*

2-6-0 '4300' class
4371, 4394, 5306, 6340, 6368, 7307.

2-6-2T '4500' class
4507, 4508, 4535, 4551, 4562, 4563, 4566, 4568, 4572, 4573, 4577, 4580, 4585, 4588, 4592, 5506-08, 5510, 5512, 5514, 5523, 5528, 5535, 5536, 5540, 5541, 5547, 5548, 5553-56, 5558, 5560, 5562-64, 5566.

4-6-0 'Hall' class
4923, *Evenley Hall*, 4945 *Milligan Hall*, 4949 *Packwood Hall*, 5969 *Honington Hall.*

2-6-2T '5100' class
5158, 5169.

TOTAL 90

ST PHILIP'S MARSH ALLOCATION 8 JANUARY 1938

2-4-0T 'Metro'
1497.

0-6-0PT '1501' class
1542.

0-6-0PT '850' class
1945, 1964, 2013, 2015.

0-6-0PT '2021' class
2044, 2070, 2072.

0-6-0 '2251' class
2251-53, 2258, 2260, 2265, 2269, 2277.

0-6-0 'Dean Goods'
2340, 2381, 2426, 2445, 2454, 2461, 2467, 2526, 2528, 2534, 2564, 2567, 2573.

0-6-0 '2361' class
2362.

2-8-0 '2800' class
2806, 2834, 2851, 2859.

2-8-0 'ROD' class
3013, 3019, 3035, 3041, 3045.

4-4-0 'Bulldog' class
3378 *River Tawe.*

0-6-0PT '8750' class
3720, 3731, 3733, 3759, 3763, 8779, 8793, 8795, 9721, 9729, 9733, 9764, 9771-73, 9784.

2-8-0T '4200' class
4221.

0-4-2T '4800' class
4836, 4854, 4855.

4-6-0 'Hall' class
4925 *Eynsham Hall*, 4956 *Plowden Hall*, 4959 *Purley Hall*, 4963 *Rignall Hall*, 4964 *Rodwell Hall*, 4969 *Shugborough Hall*, 4986 *Aston Hall*, 4992 *Crosby Hall*, 5900 *Hinderton Hall*, 5911 *Preston Hall*, 5943 *Elmdon Hall.*

2-6-2T '5101' class
5110.

2-6-2T '5100' class
5118, 5126.

Above:
Class 4F 0-6-0 No 44263 leaves Staple Hill Tunnel with a Down goods, 21 April 1960. *Author*

0-6-0PT '5700' class
5770, 5771, 5781, 5784, 5785, 7718, 7719, 7726, 7728, 7729, 7779, 7782, 7784, 7790, 7792-95, 8702, 8703, 8713, 8722, 8730, 8737, 8741.

0-4-2T '5800' class
5803, 5806, 5809.

2-6-0 '4300' class
6303, 6314, 6322, 6360, 7302, 7312, 7316, 8308, 8314, 8320.

0-6-2T '5600' class
6600.

4-6-0 'Grange' class
6804 *Brockington Grange*, 6836 *Estevarney Grange*, 6842 *Nunhold Grange*, 6859 *Yiewsley Grange*.

Total 118

BATH ROAD ALLOCATION
27 FEBRUARY 1954

4-6-0 'County' class
1005 *County of Devon*, 1007 *County of Brecknock*, 1011 *County of Chester*, 1014 *County of Glamorgan*, 1026 *County of Salop*, 1028 *County of Warwick*.

0-4-2T '1400' class
1415, 1430, 1454, 1463.

4-6-0 'Star' class
4056 *Princess Margaret*.

4-6-0 'Castle' class
4073 *Caerphilly Castle*, 4075 *Cardiff Castle*, 4084 *Aberystwyth Castle*, 4091 *Dudley Castle*, 4094 *Dynevor Castle*, 4096 *Highclere Castle*, 5000 *Launceston Castle*, 5019 *Treago Castle*, 5025 *Chirk Castle*, 5037 *Monmouth Castle*, 5048 *Earl of Devon*, 5064 *Bishop's Castle*, 5067 *St Fagans Castle*, 5069 *Isambard Kingdom Brunel*, 5074 *Hampden*, 5076 *Gladiator*, 5085 *Evesham Abbey*, 5094 *Tretower Castle*, 5096 *Bridgwater Castle*, 7011 *Banbury Castle*, 7014 *Caerhays Castle*, 7019 *Fowey Castle*, 7034 *Ince Castle*.

2-6-2T '5101' class
4139, 4157, 4159, 4166, 5182, 5197.

2-6-2T '4500' class
4532, 4535, 4558, 4577, 4582, 4592, 4595, 4597, 5506, 5512, 5514, 5523, 5525, 5528, 5532, 5535, 5546-48, 5553, 5559, 5561, 5565.

0-6-0PT '8750' class
4603, 4660, 9604, 9610.

4-6-0 'Hall' class
4909 *Blakesley Hall*, 4942 *Maindy Hall*, 4961 *Pyrland Hall*, 5904 *Kelham Hall*, 5919 *Worsley Hall*, 5949 *Trematon Hall*, 6900 *Abney Hall*, 6972 *Beningbrough Hall*, 6977 *Grundisburgh*

Hall, 6981 *Marbury Hall*, 6982 *Melmerby Hall*, 6997 *Bryn-Ivor Hall*, 7901 *Dodington Hall*, 7907 *Hart Hall.*

2-6-0 '4300' class
5307, 6351.

0-4-2T '5800' class
5809, 5813.

2-6-2T '6100' class
6107.

4-6-0 'Grange' class
6867 *Peterston Grange.*

0-6-0PT '5700' class
7782.

4-4-0 'Earl' class
9016, 9020, 9026.

TOTAL 91

ST PHILIP'S MARSH ALLOCATION 27 FEBRUARY 1954

0-6-0PT '1600' class
1649.

Below:
'Jubilee' class No 45656 *Cochrane* climbs the 1 in 63 to Fishponds with the 2.15pm Temple Meads–Birmingham New Street on 23 November 1961. *E. T. Gill/Revd Brian Arman collection*

0-6-0PT '2021' class
2053, 2070, 2072.

0-6-0 '2251' class
2203, 2215, 2250, 2251, 2261, 2265, 2269, 2293, 3215.

0-6-0 'Dean Goods'
2411.

2-8-0 '2800' class
2845, 2846, 2879, 2889, 2898, 3854.

2-8-0 'ROD' class
3014, 3017, 3032.

0-6-0PT '8750' class
3604, 3614, 3623, 3632, 3643, 3676, 3720, 3731, 3748, 3758, 3759, 3763-65, 3773, 3784, 3795, 4619, 4624, 4626, 4655, 4688, 8790, 8795, 9605, 9606, 9626, 9729, 9771.

2-8-0T '4200' class
4262.

2-8-0 '4700' class
4703, 4706.

4-6-0 'Hall' class
4914 *Cranmore Hall*, 4947 *Nanhoran Hall*, 4958 *Priory Hall*, 4983 *Albert Hall*, 4999 *Gopsal Hall*, 5924 *Dinton Hall*, 5982 *Harrington Hall*, 6908 *Downham Hall*, 6925 *Hackness Hall*, 6936 *Breccles Hall*, 6954 *Lotherton Hall*, 6957 *Norcliffe Hall*, 6958 *Oxburgh Hall*, 6986 *Rydal Hall*, 7908 *Henshall Hall.*

2-6-0 '4300' class
5306, 5325, 5350, 5351, 5367, 6322, 6363, 6370, 6374, 7303.

0-6-2T '5600' class
5675, 6601, 6656, 6670, 6671.

0-6-0PT '5700' class
5784, 7718, 7719, 7728, 7729, 7749, 7780, 7783, 7790, 7793, 7795, 8702, 8703, 8713, 8714, 8722, 8730, 8737, 8741, 8746, 8747.

4-6-0 'Grange' class
6804 *Brockington Grange*, 6811 *Cranbourne Grange*, 6827 *Llanfrechfa Grange*, 6830 *Buckenhill Grange*, 6842 *Nunhold Grange*, 6845 *Paviland Grange*, 6846 *Ruckley Grange*, 6852 *Headbourne Grange*, 6863 *Dolhywel Grange*, 6876 *Kingsland Grange*.

2-8-2T '7200' class
7201, 7250.

0-6-0PT '9400' class
8413, 8491, 8492, 9453, 9481, 9488.

0-6-0DE Class 08
13000–13003.

0-6-0DE
15100, 15107.

2-6-0 Class 2MT
46525–27.

4-6-0 Class 5MT
73019, 73022, 73027–29, 73032, 73039.

2-8-0 Class WD
90176, 90251, 90284.

ex-GWR diesel railcars
23, 24, 28, 35, 36.

TOTAL 143 PLUS 5 RAILCARS

BARROW ROAD ALLOCATION 1914

2-4-0 '1P' class
89, 90, 92, 104, 155, 178.

4-4-0 '2P' class
516–527.

4-2-2 '1P' class
607, 609, 614, 635–39, 643–45, 661–64, 669.

0-4-4T '1P' class
1228, 1331–39, 1388–90, 1397.

0-6-0T '1F' class
1870–74.

0-6-0 '1F' class
2363, 2490, 2606, 2608-10, 2632, 2665, 2724, 2829, 2833.

0-6-0 '2F' class
2988, 3071, 3072, 3074, 3076, 3077, 3079, 3087.

0-6-0 '3F' class
3155, 3156, 3159, 3193, 3194, 3400, 3593, 3594, 3615, 3621, 3712, 3713.

TOTAL 84

BARROW ROAD ALLOCATION SEPTEMBER 1935

2-4-0 '1P' class
157.

4-4-0 '2P' class
518, 520, 522-24, 629.

4-4-0 '4P' class
1023, 1025-28, 1030.

0-4-4T '1P' class
1228, 1267, 1334, 1337, 1338, 1364, 1389, 1391, 1397, 1404.

0-6-0T '1F' class
1706, 1815, 1870, 1874.

0-6-0 '2F' class
3071, 3154, 3173.

0-6-0 '3F' class
3178, 3180, 3181, 3186, 3419, 3436, 3439, 3444, 3464, 3593, 3712, 3727, 3729.

0-6-0 '4F' class
3840, 3873, 3875, 3876, 3908, 4122, 4134, 4135, 4169, 4170, 4273, 4276–78, 4424, 4533, 4534, 4535, 4536.

4-6-0 '5P5F' class
5043, 5044, 5066, 5094*–97.

0-6-0T '3F' class
7316, 16761 (7678).

2-4-0 '1P' class
20092.

TOTAL 72 * ON LOAN

BARROW ROAD ALLOCATION 30 JANUARY 1954

2-6-2T '3P' class
40116, 40120, 40164, 40174.

4-4-0 '2P' class
40426, 40486.

2-6-2T '2MT' class
41240.

0-6-0T '1F' class
41706.

0-6-0 '3F' class
43427, 43462, 43464, 43593, 43712, 43734.

0-6-0 '4F' class
43926, 43928, 43932, 43953, 44135, 44169, 44266, 44269, 44296, 44317, 44355, 44411, 44424, 44466, 44534, 44536, 44537, 44553, 44569.

4-6-0 '5MT' class
44743, 44745, 44747.

4-6-0 'Jubilee' class
45561 *Saskatchewan*, 45572 *Eire*, 45577 *Bengal*, 45602 *British Honduras*, 45651 *Shovell*, 45660 *Rooke*, 45662 *Kempenfelt*, 45663 *Jervis*, 45682 *Trafalgar*, 45685 *Barfleur*, 45690 *Leander*, 45699 *Galatea*.

0-6-0T '3F' class

47333, 47544, 47550, 47552, 47678.

0-4-0ST '0F' class

51202, 51212.

TOTAL 55

BATH ROAD ALLOCATION 17 JULY 1980

Set No	*DMUs*
Class 101/2	
805	50304, 59122, 50329.
806	50319, 59123, 50335.
Class 118/1	
460	51302, 59469, 50317.
462	51304, 59471, 51319.
465	51307, 59474, 51322.
466	51308, 59475, 51323.
467	51309, 59476, 51324.
468	51310, 59477, 51325.
469	51311, 59490, 51326.
471	51314, 59481, 51329.
472	51315, 59482, 51530.
Class 102	
800	51445, 59549, 51515.
801	51446, 59547, 51517.
802	51449, 59550, 51521.
803	51450, 59546, 51522.
804	51452, 59551, 51523.
812	51462, 59530, 51530.
813	51463, 59561, 51533.
822	51495, 59096, 51510.
820	51500, 59093, 51512.
823	51505, 59082, 51511.
821	51509, 59050, 51513.
811	51519, 59548, 51801.
810	51799, 59539, 51808.
Class 121	
132	55032
133	55033

Class 50 Co-Co

50039–044

Class 31 A1A-A1A

31118, 31123, 31128, 31131, 31136, 31145, 31154, 31159, 31165, 31170, 31210, 31231, 31258, 31286, 31294, 31296, 31307, 31401, 31419–424.

Class 47 Co-Co

47001, 47008, 47020, 47026, 47032, 47035, 47083, 47091, 47095, 47099, 47101, 47129, 47136–138, 47140, 47142, 47152, 47159, 47244–252, 47267, 47282–286, 47293, 47327.

Class 37 Co-Co

37158, 37159, 37203–208, 37210, 37224, 37231–233, 37241, 37295.

Class 03 0-6-0

03121, 03382.

Class 08 0-6-0

08185, 08218, 08338, 08363, 08483, 08491, 08643, 08668, 08756, 08800, 08821, 08900, 08935, 08942, 08950, 08951.

TOTALS: TWO SINGLE-CAR DMUS
24 THREE-CAR DMUS
99 LOCOMOTIVES

ST PHILIP'S MARSH ALLOCATION 19 JANUARY 1996

Class 08 0-6-0

08410, 08483, 08643, 08836.

Class 47 Co-Co

47811, 47815, 47816, 47832 *Tamar*

Class 43 HST Power Car Bo-Bo

43002 *Top of the Pops*, 43003, 43004, 43005, 43009, 43010, 43011 *Reader 125*, 40312, 40315, 43016 *Bristol Bath Road*, 43017, 43018, 43019 *Dinas Abertawe/City of Swansea*, 43020 *John Grooms*, 43021, 43022, 43023 *County of Cornwall*, 43024, 43025 *Exeter*, 43026 *City of Westminster*, 43027 *Glorious Devon*, 43030, 43031, 43032 *The Royal Regiment of Wales*, 43033, 43034 *The Black Horse*, 43035, 43036, 43037, 43040 *Granite City*, 43124, 43125 *Merchant Venturer*, 43126 *City of Bristol*, 43127, 43128, 43129, 43130 *Sulis Minerva*, 43131 *Sir Felix Pole*, 43132 *Worshipful Company of Carmen*, 43133, 43134 *County of Somerset*, 43135, 43136, 43137, 43138, 43139, 43140, 43141, 43142, 43143, 43144, 43145, 43146, 43147 *The Red Cross*, 43148, 43149 *BBC Wales Today*, 43150 *Bristol Evening Post*, 43151, 43152 *St Peters School York AD627*, 43163, 43168, 43169 *The National Trust*, 43170 *Edward Paxman*, 43171, 43172, 43173, 43174, 43175, 43176, 43177 *University of Exeter*, 43179 *Pride of Laira*, 43181 *Devonport Royal Dockyard 1693–1993*, 43182, 43183, 43185 *Great Western*, 43186 *Sir Francis Drake*, 43187, 43188 *City of Plymouth*, 43189 *Railway Heritage Trust*, 43190, 43191 *Seahawk*, 43192 *City of Truro*

TOTALS: 82 HST POWER CARS
EIGHT LOCOMOTIVES

BIBLIOGRAPHY

Ahrons, E. L. — *Locomotive & Train Working in the Latter Part of the Nineteenth Century:* Vols 2 and 4; Heffer, 1952

Allen, C. J. — *Titled Trains of the Western*; Ian Allan Ltd, 1974

Allen, G. F. — *The Western Since 1948*; Ian Allan Ltd, 1979

Arrowsmith, J. W. — *Dictionary of Bristol*; Bristol, 1906

Buchanan, R. A. and Cossons, N. — *The Industrial Archaeology of the Bristol Region*; David & Charles, 1969

Clinker, C. R. — *Closed Stations & Goods Depots*; Avon Anglia, 1988

Clinker, C. R. — 'Railway Development at Bristol', *Railway Magazine*; September, October, November 1956

Cocks, R. H. — 'Notable Railway Stations: Temple Meads', *Railway Magazine*; October 1900

Cooke, R. A. — *Track Layout Diagrams of the GWR and BR WR Section 19*; Author 1975 and 1992

Cornock, W. — 'Railway Warehouses and Goods Depots', *Railway & Travel Monthly*; June 1914

Cullen, E. — 'Industrial Development by Railways: Canon's Marsh Extension', *Great Western Railway Magazine*; June 1906

Fellows, Canon R. B. — 'Rival Routes to Bristol', *Railway World*; November/December 1960

Fleming, D. J. — *St Philip's Marsh*; Bradford Barton, 1980

Hately, R. — *Industrial Locomotives of South Western England*; Industrial Railway Society, 1977

Hawkins, C. & Reeve, G. — *LMS Engine Sheds Vol 2*; Wild Swan, 1981.

Kichenside, G. M. — 'WR's £4 million Bristol Resignalling Plan', *Modern Railways*; July 1968

Latimer, J. — *Annals of Bristol in the Nineteenth Century*; Bristol, 1887.

Leleux, S. A. — *Brotherhoods, Engineers*; David & Charles, 1965

Lyons, E. and Mountford, E. — *An Historical Survey of Great Western Engine Sheds 1947*; Oxford Publishing Co, 1972

Lyons, E. — *An Historical Survey of Great Western Engine Sheds 1837–1947*; Oxford Publishing Co, 1974

MacDermot, E. T./Clinker, C. R. and Nock, O. S. — *History of the Great Western Railway*; Ian Allan Ltd, 1964/1967

Maggs, C. G. — *Bristol Railway Panorama*; Millstream, 1990

Maggs, C. G. — *The Bristol & Gloucester Railway*; Oakwood Press, 1992

Maggs, C. G. — *The Mangotsfield to Bath Branch*; Oakwood Press, 1992

Below:
In semi-rural surroundings new Fiat cars await unloading at the Chittening Estate Siding, 7 March 1996. *Author*

Maggs, C. G. — *The Bristol Port Railway & Pier*; Oakwood Press, 1975

Maggs, C. G. — 'The Railways between Bristol and Bath', *Railway World*; February, March, April 1960

Neale, W. G. — *At the Port of Bristol*; Port of Bristol Authority, 1970

Nock, O. S. — 'Resorts for Railfans, Bristol', *Trains Illustrated*; May 1952

Oakley, M. — *Railway Stations & Halts in Avon*; Avon County Council, 1984

Oakley, M. — *Bristol Suburban*; Redcliffe Press, 1990

Pell-Hiley, A. G. — 'Twenty Four Hours at Bristol', *Railway Magazine*; October 1909

Railway Correspondence & Travel Society; *Locomotives of the Great Western Railway, Parts 1–14*, RCTS 1952-93

Rust, C. R. — 'A Stationmaster's Day at Bristol Temple Meads', *Railway Magazine*; September 1959

Vaughan, A. — *A Pictorial Record of Great Western Architecture*; Oxford Publishing Co, 1977

Vaughan, A. — *A Pictorial Record of Great Western Signalling*; Oxford Publishing Co, 1973

Vincent, M. — *Lines to Avonmouth*; Oxford Publishing Co, 1979

Vincent, M. — *Reflections on the Portishead Branch*; Oxford Publishing Co, 1983

Warnock, D. W. — *The Bristol & North Somerset Railway 1863–1884*; Temple Cloud, 1978

Warnock, D. W. & Parsons, R. G. — *The Bristol & North Somerset Railway since 1884*; Avon Anglia, 1979

Warburton, M. B. — 'Serving the Port of Bristol', *Railway Magazine*; August 1972

Whitley, H. S. — 'The Canon's Marsh Extension, Bristol', *Great Western Railway Magazine*; July 1906

Anon; 'Bristol as a Railway Centre', *Modern Transport*; May 1924

Anon; 'The Bristol Division of the Great Western Railway', *Railway Gazette*; May 1924

Anon; 'New Works at Bristol', *Engineer*; January 1907

Above:
Class 9F 2-10-0 No 92238 at Barrow Road, 30 June 1955. A wagon turntable is on the left and in the background is the water softener, left, and the brick-built engine shed, right. *Revd Alan Newman*